Gillian

SPRINGSONG ❧ BOOKS

Andrea

Anne

Carrie

Colleen

Cynthia

Gillian

Jenny

Joanna

Kara

Kathy

Lisa

Melissa

Michelle

Paige

Sherri

Gillian

Laurel Oke Logan

BETHANY HOUSE PUBLISHERS
MINNEAPOLIS, MINNESOTA 55438

Gillian
Laurel Oke Logan

Library of Congress Catalog Card Number 86–70911

ISBN 1–55661–681–3

SpringSong edition published 1995
Copyright © 1986
Laurel Oke Logan

Published by Bethany House Publishers
A Ministry of Bethany Fellowship, Inc.
11300 Hampshire Avenue South
Minneapolis, Minnesota 55438

Printed in the United States of America

To Gene
To Deborah Morgan

LAUREL OKE LOGAN, the daughter of Janette Oke, was born and raised in Canada. Laurel is a homemaker, a writer, and the mother of four children. She and her husband, Marvin, make their home in Indiana.

1

"And so, fellow students, we have a choice." Gillian watched herself in the mirror as she practiced. She wanted this speech to be just right.

"Gillian," a voice from downstairs called, "we have to leave in ten minutes. Are you just about ready?"

"Yes, Mom," Gillian answered. Ten minutes was hardly enough time to run through the whole speech, she thought anxiously. Maybe she should just practice the parts that had most recently changed. Her pounding heart made it difficult to concentrate.

"This choice can be likened to that of a man who has a city bus token." Gillian resumed her practice. "He may use this token to travel near or far, depending on his ambition. Should he so choose, the token may take him only to the next corner. However, if he raises his sights, he may travel a great distance and accomplish much.

"We also possess a token. Our diploma is a token of the growing and learning that have helped to shape us. We must use this token to travel as far as we can. We must take the first step, believing we can achieve any goal we set for ourselves."

She lifted her eyes again to the mirror in front of her, scrutinizing her face. Somehow she didn't think she looked like a valedictorian. Maybe she should pull her hair up instead of letting it fall freely down her back. No, that always made her look like a little girl playing dress-up. She forced her attention back to her speech.

"My challenge to you, then, is to be daring. Do not set a goal for your life that is easily attained. Too quickly we settle back into unfulfilling lifestyles because we are afraid to leave our familiar surroundings. Don't allow routine to govern your endeavors. Rather, set your sights on a distant objective. Then, when your journey is complete, you will be able to look back and say, 'I have succeeded. I am satisfied.' Thank you."

Applause echoed throughout the auditorium. For a brief second she lingered in the glory of the moment, pride radiating from her soft green eyes. Then slowly she returned to her seat, clutching her notes tightly in a trembling hand, nearly covered by the long full sleeve of her graduation gown.

The dreadful waiting followed as each impatient student was awarded a diploma, proud parents beaming in the audience. It was a day to remember.

With exaggerated dignity, Principal Quigley approached the microphone and raised his hand to signal for silence. "Ladies and gentlemen, it is with great pride that I present to you this year's graduating class." A cheer rose from the floor, along with a cloud of graduation caps as the graduates were released at last from the lengthy ceremonies.

"Hey, Jill," a voice cried out above the voices and laughter all around. It was Krystal. The chubby blonde pushed her way through the mass of people, as oblivious to them as they were to her.

"Good speech, Jill! You really sounded scholarly."

"Thanks, Krystal," Gillian answered with a grin.

"Where'd you get the idea for the bus token?"

"Oh," mused Gillian, "I was just tired of the old 'education is a key to open the door of life' bit so I added a different twist. Do you think it worked?"

"Yes. It even caught Mr. Quigley's attention," Krystal affirmed.

"That's all I wanted. Every year he sits and nods piously through the whole valedictorial speech and I decided that I didn't want him doing that while I was giving mine. Everybody knows that he isn't even listening. Well, it's a small victory but at least it's something."

As Krystal tried to pry her way through the crowd, she added, "Maybe you should have just taught him to say your name right. You'd think that after four years he would know to pronounce Gillian with a 'J' sound instead of a hard 'G.' Every time he says *Gh*illian I think of a fish."

The two girls had now reached the rest of their friends, and they all began discussing the ceremonies.

"Can you believe Clint Johnson! When he told me he wasn't going to wear anything under his robe, I didn't believe him. I could have died when he walked up there with his bare feet and boney ankles sticking out from under his robe."

"*You* could have died? I thought Mr. Quigley was really going to fall over! It looked like he wasn't sure whether to give Clint his diploma just to get him off stage or kick him out of school. I heard he was wearing swimming trunks, though."

"I guess you're not the only one who wanted to make a lasting impression on old Quigley, Jill," Krystal added heartily. "Hey, guys, how about our Jill? When's the last time you heard a valedictorian who was actually creative about her speech?"

"Yeah, Gillian," Janet said, stepping forward. "Your speech was really great. I think some of the guys even listened."

"Don't say that, Janet," Rob blurted out in an effort to sound offended. "We'll lose our image if you go spreading rumors."

"Tony doesn't have to worry about his image. Did you all hear his stomach growl? Man, it was loud!"

"Knock it off, Kevin," Tony muttered, giving Kevin a rough shove.

"Speaking of being hungry," Rob said, trying to change the subject, "why don't we all stop over at my house for something to eat? My mom bought doughnuts yesterday, and I'm sure she'd appreciate it if we get rid of them for her."

"Sure, Rob, we're willing to help her out," Tony was quick to answer.

"Then let's go."

———

High school quickly became a fading memory to Gillian as she and her friends moved into the rigors of college life. Attending the small local college seemed like an insignificant step forward, but the years spent there went quickly. Soon they found themselves again walking proudly down the long aisle to receive their diplomas.

After the ceremonies, Gillian and her friends relaxed in Tony's dorm room. Since Tony had already completed most of his packing, the walls were bare and boxes crowded the floor, making movement difficult.

None of them seemed bothered by the mess, however, and they chatted easily while they ate one last pizza together and toasted one another's success with cans of Coke.

"Hey, Rob," Kevin asked between mouthfuls, "how'd that new job offer turn out?"

"Not bad," Rob replied. "They took me out and showed me the city and plant. I felt like a king the way they treated me. First-class plane ticket, deluxe hotel room— even my own rental car. I went for interviews with three of the managers whose departments I'm being considered for. I think I'd be happy working for any one of them. How'd *your* interviews go?"

"Not as well as that, but I'm happy. Triple-Com Products is a pretty small business right now, but they'll grow a lot in the near future. I want my wallet right in there growing along with them, if you know what I mean."

"Sure we do, Kevin," Krystal cut in. "You engineers aren't the only ones who have big plans. We nurses have some goals, too. Memorial has offered me a managing position and I intend to take it. There's not a better hospital in this city."

"Hey, Gillian," Kevin continued, "how are your interviews turning out?"

Caught off guard, Gillian shrugged, trying to brush the question aside. Her mind raced for some sort of reply. There was no way that she would admit how discouraged she felt. A quick and subtle lie formed on her lips. "I'm doing okay so far, but I haven't made any definite plans yet. It's not easy to choose just which job to take." The truth was, Gillian had not yet received a job offer from any of the places where she had interviewed. It was not that she wasn't wanted. It was simply that, in the area close by, there were not many restaurant and hotel management positions available. She had spent many hours driving from interview to interview, but had little to show for her efforts. All she had heard was that they had nothing yet, but if there was an opening, she was the first on the list. To Gillian, who needed a good job to pay off college loans, this news was devastating.

"Janet got a good offer," Krystal piped in. She knew Gillian's situation and was trying to change the subject.

Janet blushed for a moment and then let the others pressure her to explain her good fortune. "I've been offered an accounting position at Society Bank and Trust. Everyone said that a business person needs to be pushy to succeed, but I guess I proved that wrong. I'm sure not the pushy type. Intelligence does still count for something."

"You should try that approach sometime, Kevin," Krystal teased.

Everyone laughed. The topic changed to lighter subjects of the year's highlights and moving home.

Gillian was the only one who found it difficult to enter

into their light conversation. Her thoughts were still on her personal dilemma of finding a good job. How would she ever find a job immediately when she had tried all semester and failed? She could always work in the flower shop where she had worked each summer since high school. They would surely hire her back, but it would be such a waste of her college education.

Maybe she hadn't looked for a job in the right places, but where else could she look? Gillian had tried all the places in the small city she knew by reputation. She had even gone through the telephone book.

"Hey, Gillian, are you with us or what?" Kevin's voice broke into her thoughts, bringing her attention back to the people around her.

"Sorry, I'm just a little drained, I guess. I'm going back to the dorm to turn in. I'll see you guys later."

Her vague excuse was quickly accepted and the group returned to its chatter, but Krystal followed Gillian to the door.

"Are you all right, Jill?" she questioned, eyeing her carefully.

"Sure I am," Gillian replied as emphatically as she could. "I'm just a little bushed. Go on back in there and have fun. And don't worry about me. I'll be okay if I just get some sleep."

"Well, if you're sure," Krystal said cautiously. "I'll see you tomorrow then."

———

The next day Gillian packed up and drove home, but she still couldn't shake the depression that had settled over her the night before. Cars seemed to be everywhere on that Sunday, pushing and shoving each other to fit into crowded restaurant parking lots. Gillian wondered what it would be like to go to church every Sunday and then out to eat. It seemed like the ritual used up a lot of time—time that could be spent sleeping in or relaxing at home. As she moved out of the downtown area, she tried to plan a new strategy.

I haven't applied in Clancy's Bar yet, she thought. *I'd always pictured myself in a classier place, but it could be a start. Maybe from there I could move to a nicer restaurant. I hope it doesn't take too long.* Then she muttered to herself, "Imagine, a high-school valedictorian graduating from college and ending up working in a bar. What a reward for four years of hard work."

As soon as Gillian arrived home, she hurried to the backyard where she knew her father would be working. Maybe he could come up with a better idea.

"Well, Gillian," Mr. Todd greeted her warmly, looking up from his work, "it's so nice to have you back home for good."

"I guess I'm glad it's over," she answered. "What are you doing?"

"Your mother got it into her head that we needed some rosebushes along this fence. Now I'm the one who has to fight with the prickly things. Isn't that just like a woman?" As he spoke he straightened, brushing the dirt from his knees, and turned to face Gillian. Seeing her pensive expression, he quickly added, "What's wrong, angel?"

Gillian sighed deeply. "Daddy, it's just that I don't have a job yet, and everyone else seems to. I'm getting pretty miserable thinking about it."

"Well then, you can stop being miserable. I have good news. I've been doing some poking around on my own for you, and I think I've found something wonderful." Gillian breathed a quick sigh of relief. She knew that her father wouldn't let her down.

"It just so happens that Ed Jeffery called yesterday and said his daughter and son-in-law have a camp up in Canada and are looking for someone to manage the kitchen." The blood drained from Gillian's face. "They just lost their last manager and need a new person to take over just as soon as possible. I think it's a perfect opportunity for you, and it certainly wouldn't hurt you to get off on your own for a while. You've lived too long in the confines of this little city. Besides, it's the area of Canada where your mother and I used to live when you were very young. I always hoped you'd get to live there again."

"Canada!" Gillian exclaimed. "You can't be serious. Surely there's something a whole lot closer than that."

"It wouldn't be so bad," her father assured her. "It's beautiful in that area of the Rockies and the job is in a very plush, expensive resort. There have to be a lot of bucks floating around a place like that."

Don't be ridiculous! Gillian wanted to shout back. Instead, she bit her lip and tried to answer him evenly. After all, he had only been trying to help. "I don't want to leave, Dad. Especially to go that far."

"I know you don't, sugar, but you haven't found anything at all in this area. If you don't make a decision soon, even this job will be gone, and I sincerely doubt you'll get another opportunity like this. The man who used to work there left to manage a really fancy restaurant in Chicago. They say this place will be a terrific plus on your resumé. And it would be nice for you to see the place where you were born. Remember, you're as much a Canadian as you are an American with your dual citizenship."

"Daddy, I don't remember Canada at all. You and Mom left there when I was only two and I've never been back. All the legal papers might declare me part Canadian, but you know my heart is here. Besides," Gillian finished weakly, "I was thinking I'd try a few more places around here."

"Where could you apply that you haven't tried already?"

Gillian bit her lip and mumbled, "I heard that Clancy's might need someone."

"No way!" Mr. Todd thundered. "No daughter of mine

is going to work in a roach-infested hole like Clancy's. Gillian, you can't be serious. Surely I've raised you with more sense than that."

"It's not that bad," Gillian answered as a tear trickled down one cheek. "I don't know what else to try, Daddy."

Mr. Todd softened and reached for her, pulling her close to his chest. "Don't cry, sugar," he soothed, stroking her hair with his work-worn hand. "I'm not saying that you have to take the job in Canada, but I want you to at least give it some serious thought. Will you promise me that?"

"Okay," sniffed Gillian. "I'll think about it. But please don't stop looking around here. I really don't want to leave."

"Promise," he answered.

Gillian straightened and pulled herself away. She rubbed at her eyes where she knew her mascara had smudged and tried to smile. How could things have gone so wrong? This wasn't right. She was supposed to be able to choose what she wanted to do with her life. Suddenly it seemed that her fate had already been decided and there was nothing she could do to change it. A quiet dread crept into her heart, and somehow she knew the inevitable.

"Go see your mother now," prodded Mr. Todd. "She's been anxious to see you all morning."

Slowly Gillian turned and ambled toward the gray-blue house. Without feeling, she opened the sliding glass door and entered the dining room of her parents' two-story home.

"Gillian, is that you?" a high-pitched voice called from the upper floor.

"Yes, Mom," she called back.

In a moment her mother was hugging her close and welcoming her home.

"Did you talk to your father?" she began at once.

Not you, too, Gillian thought defeatedly and then answered, "Yes, he told me about the job."

"What do you think?"

"What am I supposed to think?" she grumbled. "There doesn't seem to be any other choice, does there?"

"Don't be so discouraged. Nobody's trying to run your life for you. You can say no if you want to."

"Sure, Mom, and then what would I do? Collect unemployment insurance until I'm sixty and I can retire?"

"It's not that bad," Mrs. Todd stated frankly. "Your father told me about the camp and it sounds delightful."

"What did he say about it?" Gillian sighed.

"It's supposed to be a retreat for harassed businessmen who want to escape to the wilderness for a while. I think he said that it's near Banff, but I'm not really sure about that. It is in British Columbia, though—in the mountains. Your father has always wished that you could see the mountains. Ever since we left Alberta to move south, he's wanted to go back. This is a chance for him to send something of himself back to his country, and I guess he's pretty excited about the idea."

"I know he feels that way, Mom, but I'm finding it hard to share his excitement. It's his world that he left, not mine. I don't think I'd fit in very well at all."

"Shouldn't you give it a chance?" Gillian's mother prodded gently.

It did sound interesting, but she wasn't sure if she liked the idea of being stuck in the middle of the mountains with only misplaced businessmen around her. She could hardly believe that these men would be good company, and the thought of living so far from her home still frightened her.

The idea of living in the mountains, however, did rather appeal to her. She had seen pictures of the Rockies and they looked inviting enough, but she just wasn't sure if she would be satisfied with the life there. She was used to the comforts of the city. She enjoyed going to the shopping mall, the movies, and her friends' houses as often as she wanted. In the mountains there would be none of these, except perhaps a friend's house or two if she happened to be lucky enough to find a suitable friend among all those rugged men. Making friends had never been an issue. There had never been any need for her to learn how. All her life she had been surrounded by people who knew and loved her. It would be a difficult adjustment to make, one she wasn't sure she was ready for.

"Well, dear," Mrs. Todd cut into her thoughts, "you think it over for a while. It's a big decision." Then she added with a sigh, "I have to run to a women's meeting. Will you find something for you and your father to eat for dinner while I change out of these jeans? There should be leftovers in the fridge."

"Sure," Gillian answered amiably.

"Thanks," came the reply as her mother started down the hall. Gillian was alone again with her turbulent thoughts.

———

That night Gillian lay turning the idea over in her head until she heard the front door softly open and close. Her mother had returned from the meeting at last. It was late, but Gillian decided to get up. She certainly hadn't been able to sleep. As she stepped into the hall, her mother motioned her to follow without making any noise.

When they had arrived downstairs, Mrs. Todd turned with an inquisitive look. "Why are you still awake? Can't you sleep?"

"I keep thinking about that management position in Canada. I can't decide whether to take it or not."

"Gillian, we certainly don't want to pressure you into anything you don't want. Your father just feels that he knows what's best, and you can't blame him for wanting only the best for you."

"I'm glad he cares enough to want to push me when he thinks he knows what's right. I'm just not convinced that you have to live in the mountains for part of your life in order to be a complete person. I like it where I am. Guess that doesn't matter, though. It's getting pretty clear that I can't stay around here and work too. I suppose that I may as well go along with Dad's idea since I'm going to have to move. But Canada's so far away."

"There's nothing wrong with stepping out on your own. For a lot of people it builds character, but it's got to be what you want. If you leave with the wrong attitude—or have any doubt at all, for that matter—you might as well stay at home. You'll only be miserable. If you're going to take a step as big as that, it had better be what you want and you'd better be willing to give it an honest effort. Do you think you'll be able to do that?"

"I don't know, Mom," Gillian answered honestly, "I don't know enough about it to make that choice yet."

"Maybe the best thing to do would be to give Mr. Jeffery a call and ask him about it. Then we'll find out who we can get in touch with at the camp and you can ask any questions Ed couldn't answer."

Gillian thought for a moment. "Thanks, Mom," she grinned, leaning forward to give her a hug. "I really needed some good, sound advice right now. I finally feel like I can do something constructive about my future."

"Well, you're certainly welcome," Mrs. Todd said and then added, "I have a lot of faith in you, Gillian. I'm sure you'll make the right decision—either way."

2

For Gillian, the next week was hectic. She called Mr. Jeffery and, after more careful consideration, put in a long-distance call to British Columbia, Canada. The information she gained from each of these telephone calls began to sway her toward accepting the job. It truly did sound promising. She was very impressed with the things she had been told about the camp. It had been established only a few short years ago but became popular immediately, not only in that area of the country, but to men as far away as Ontario and even some parts of the United States. The place offered a unique opportunity to be close to nature, and yet provided many of the modern conveniences that Gillian would have found hard to give up. There were crude cabins without running water or electric heat, but there was also an elaborate lodge for anyone who felt he could not be comfortable while "roughing it."

Gillian planned to stay in the lodge, but she decided against telling her father. He might have other ideas. She imagined all the things she would have to give up if she stayed in a cabin. Her hair wouldn't be a problem since it was short and straight. But what would she do on a cold winter morning without even a blow-dryer or an electric blanket at night?

Gillian had felt the pressure build when she made the call to the camp and Mr. Phillips, the owner, said they needed someone immediately. Mr. Phillips had asked that she plan to arrive by the following Monday. Could she really be ready to move to another country in less than a week? She wasn't sure.

On Wednesday Krystal stopped by and Gillian filled her in on the details. Amazed that so much could happen in three short days, Krystal did not hesitate to give her opinion on the matter.

"As I see it, you have two options," she said, trying to sound as wise as she could. "You can stay around here and spend your summer frantically looking for a job, or you can take the Canadian one and settle back into the life of making money rather than spending it. Besides, you're not signing a life contract or anything. If you really don't like the job, you can always come back. What is there to lose?"

"My dignity, if nothing else." Gillian tossed back and then sighed, "It's not hard to tell what side of the road you're on."

"I'm a woman of definite opinion. One of those opinions just happens to be that my friends should succeed and be happy with their lives. What's so wrong with that?"

"Nothing at all, except when you make sense, it makes it more difficult to decide."

After Krystal had gone, Gillian went to her room to sort things out again. The money was good. The offer was promising. The experience would probably be valuable for her. The opportunity seemed too good to give up. So what was stopping her? Fear. Some fear eating away at her confidence, making her believe the decision would change her whole life. Krystal had said she could always come back if she didn't like it. Maybe her fear was that she might not ever want to. What then? It was very difficult for Gillian to picture herself never coming back home.

In the end fear lost out and Gillian knew she would take the job. On Thursday she again found herself on the phone talking with Mr. Phillips. She accepted the job, determined that it would only last for one short year. After she had hung up, she sighed. So it was settled. She would travel all day Monday and reach the camp late that night.

Gillian soon found, however, that making the decision was only the beginning. Her father immediately had her call the airline and reserve a seat. Then he sat down with her and made a list of all the things she would need to purchase in order to accommodate a colder climate. Mr. Phillips had said the dress code in the kitchen would be casual since the men who stayed there expected everything to be simple and rugged. But Gillian's father was determined that what she already owned would not do.

Gillian spent the rest of the day with her mother, going from shop to shop, filling all the needs on the list. The large number of purchases was mind-boggling to her and she wondered if it was really necessary or if her parents were just trying to feel involved by helping her with the extra purchases and attention.

Outfit after outfit was laid on the counter of each store. Usually Gillian would have been very excited at all the new things, thrilling at the idea of wearing each for the first time. Her mind refused to swell with excitement, however. Her thoughts kept returning to one question: Would there be anyone at the camp to see and appreciate her new clothes? No, she decided sadly, no one would care whether she wore expensive jeans or a grubby old pair from college days. Nor would anyone notice how well the rugged flannel shirts contrasted with her finely featured face, making her look more feminine than ever.

That evening she finally had a chance to slow down and think things through as she folded her new wardrobe and placed each piece into her suitcases. Her decision was binding now, and yet her doubts had not diminished. In fact, they were stronger than ever. Early Monday morning she would leave on a plane to a country she had only seen as a child and in pictures. Would it be at all like the impression those photos had given or would she find many things no one wanted to take pictures of?

The last three days seemed to stretch into eternity. The nights grew longer as she spent more time waking and thinking about her new destiny.

Finally Monday arrived and she drove to the local airport with her parents. The day was unusually cool and gloomy, perfectly reflective of how Gillian felt. Both of her parents tried to act casual and unaffected, but their efforts were futile.

"Don't forget to wear your jacket when you get off the plane. It may be T-shirt weather here, but it's a lot cooler in the mountains. You'll need to be prepared."

"Sure, Mom," Gillian smiled halfheartedly.

Mr. Todd turned to her, looking very uncomfortable about saying goodbye. "Don't forget that we love you, angel. We'll be expecting to hear from you often. It doesn't take long to write a letter and it will be very important to us now."

You were the one that wanted me to go so badly, Gillian thought to herself. *Now you look as pitiful as the rest of us. That does a whole lot for my confidence.*

"You're sure you know which plane to catch in Chicago and what gate to board from?"

"I wrote it all down and, besides, you've quizzed me so many times I think I have it memorized."

"Honey, we're only trying to help," Mrs. Todd pleaded tensely.

"I know, Mom. And I don't mean to sound ungrateful. You've both been really kind and I appreciate your support."

"That's what parents are for," her father stated emphatically.

At that moment a voice came over the intercom system

giving the first boarding call for Gillian's flight. She quickly hugged her parents and gathered her carry-on bag to board the plane.

"If there's anything that you need, don't hesitate to call."

"I know, Dad," she said, then headed for the gate. She gave her parents one more look before stepping onto the ramp, calling out, "I love you!" She was now turning away from everything familiar and walking toward the unknown.

It was the first time Gillian had taken such a major step alone. Even when she had gone to her hometown college, she and Krystal had stalked the campus the year before, finding every secret path and corner in the entire area. By the time classes began, it was all old hat to her.

She supposed this experience was long overdue, but the knowledge didn't seem to settle her churning stomach. The plane suddenly looked menacing and the ramp beneath her felt unstable. After she had taken her seat, she looked out the window and saw her parents searching for her. She waved, but they didn't see her.

The flight was short, taking her only to Chicago where she was to board the next plane. Even after her father's constant coaching, it was a difficult process. There were so many people that it was hard for her to move forward, let alone try to watch above her for signs pointing to the needed airline.

Just as she was about to cry in frustration, Gillian spotted the desk for Air Canada and hurried in behind the waiting people. The line in front of her inched slowly forward while Gillian shifted nervously from foot to foot, not certain that she was yet where she belonged. At last it was her turn to step up to the desk.

Gillian soon realized that, because of the time change, she had two hours to wait for her next plane. Finding a small ice cream shop, she ordered a Coke and read the book she had brought along. The time flew by and soon she was on the airplane taxiing out to the runway. She again felt a thrill as the plane rushed forward and drifted effortlessly from the earth below. Now that she was actually on her way, she settled into the seat and relaxed. The time spent reading had made her feel much more calm and composed. She even talked with the lady next to her for a while, something she usually found very difficult. Somehow, a strange spirit of adventure crept into her, making her feel bold and daring. After about three hours, when the plane coasted in for a landing, Gillian was completely calm.

From the Calgary airport, Gillian took a taxi to the bus station. The bus would then take her to a small town close to the camp itself where her ride would be waiting. Since it would be a few hours until the bus would leave, Gillian used the time to stroll down the streets near the station. She picked up several interesting postcards and then found a quiet restaurant where she ate dinner and jotted short notes on the cards to each of her friends.

The sky had already turned deep gray by the time Gillian returned to the depot. She boarded the bus, then waited impatiently for it to leave the crowded station. At last its engines raced and the bus pressed forward, entering the streams of traffic on the highway and leaving the city lights behind. She was surprised that she could be so tired after sitting for what had seemed an eternity, but the gentle motion of the bus as it sped through the gathering night rocked her to sleep. In seemingly no time at all, she woke to see a large sign flash by the window: "Welcome to the friendly town of Linden."

Although it was already late at night, the street lights revealed the town around her. The road they'd come in on passed little more than the bus depot as it continued around a sharp bend. Trees crowded in on all sides. Gillian was amazed that the town was so small.

The words "Are you Miss Todd?" met her and pulled her from her reflections as she stepped down from the bus.

"Yes, I'm Gillian," she answered quickly.

"My name is Kate Phillips," said a small woman with dark hair and soft features. As she smiled up at Gillian her cheeks wrinkled into dimples and laugh lines. Gillian knew immediately that she would like Kate, but a familiar awkwardness settled over her.

"It's good to meet you, Mrs. Phillips," Gillian replied, trying not to show how nervous she had become. After all, this was her new employer.

"Oh, call me Kate," came the quick answer. " 'Mrs.' sounds much too formal. I hope your trip was all right. I'm sorry for the long, late bus ride, but it's one of the few ways we have of getting people out here. You're probably very tired, but it won't take us long to get back to the camp and then we'll get you settled."

As she spoke, Kate scooped up Gillian's suitcases and rushed them off to the waiting car. Gillian had to trot to keep up with her quick pace.

The hurried antics of the outgoing woman put Gillian at ease. "I didn't mind the trip so much," Gillian assured her. "I was so tired that I slept most of the way."

"I understand that. Traveling is tiresome and I am sorry we had to rush your trip so much, but if you could see our schedule, you would understand our time pressures," Kate said emphatically. "I tried to run the kitchen myself, but I'm not much of an authority figure. People just don't take me seriously when I try to tell them what to do. I guess that's the way it is with short people."

Gillian laughed and climbed in beside Kate. The car rumbled for a moment and then shot out into the black night. With Kate at the wheel, it was not long before they were driving into camp and Gillian was being shown to her cabin. The camp was dark and, although Gillian strained to make out the forms around her as she stumbled after Kate along the dirt trail, she could recognize very little.

"Here's your cabin," Kate announced as she opened the door to a small rust-colored building.

Gillian stepped inside and jumped in surprise when Kate flipped on the light switch. So there was electricity after all. "It's nice, Kate, but—" she began as she glanced behind her, intending to tell Kate that she would rather stay in the lodge. Kate had already gone to get the suitcases from outside the door. After one more look around, Gillian decided not to bother Kate with her request that night. Tomorrow she would move to the lodge.

"I know you're tired, so I'll leave you alone," Kate babbled as soon as she had returned. "I'm sure you're worn out from your day and there's lots of time tomorrow to talk business." Kate turned quickly to leave and then added with a wink, "I'm glad you're here, Gillian. I can tell we're going to get along just fine. Have a good sleep."

As soon as Kate had gone, Gillian sized up her cabin. It was small, divided into two rooms, but looked clean and comfortable. The walls and floor were roughly finished. The main door was set off to the right at the front of the cabin. To the left of this door was a small round table with two wooden chairs set directly in front of a window. The curtains were made of soft calico with dainty yellow and green flowers, giving the front room a cheerful look. Gillian was pleased. Toward the back of the room, directly in front of the entry door, was a small wood-burning stove and a cushioned chair. On the wall to the far left of the room was a bookshelf with a few books, leaving plenty of room for the things she had brought with her. Above the shelf was one precious electrical outlet. Several rugs scattered here and there gave the room a rustic but cozy appearance.

The door into the bedroom was beside the bookshelf. As she entered the room, she first noticed the large, comfortable-looking bed covered with a heavy quilt. There was also a nightstand beside the bed and a large dresser with a mirror. There was no closet, but as she hadn't brought any dresses to hang in it she knew it wouldn't be missed.

Suddenly she laughed. "Why am I looking so carefully?" she sputtered aloud. "It doesn't matter if there's a closet or not because I'm going to stay in the lodge. I'm acting as if I actually planned to live here." Gillian glanced quickly around the room one last time and then sank carelessly onto the bed. The downy quilt cradled her slim form. Not until then did Gillian realize how tired she was. The bed felt so inviting that in no time at all she had slipped into a cotton nightgown, placed her contact lenses carefully in their containers on the dresser, and was sleeping peacefully under the cottony warmth of the comforter.

3

The next morning Gillian woke with a start, at first having an unnerving feeling of not knowing where she was. Soon she remembered everything and slipped out from under the sheltered warmth of the soft bed. The floor felt icy cold under her feet and the room quite chilly so she dressed quickly, shivering as she pulled a heavy olive-colored sweater over her tousled hair. She wanted to freshen up, but didn't remember seeing any place to do that in her cabin.

As she entered the front room, she spied a metal basin with some water in it set toward the back of the stove. The water was cold but she supposed it would have to do. There was certainly no way she wanted to struggle with a fire.

After she had washed as best she could, she stepped back into the bedroom and finished getting ready for the first day on her new job. She found her makeup case, and in a few minutes, even in the shadowed mirror, her complexion shone back rosy and bright, her green eyes sparkling with life. She tossed the case back onto her pile of folded clothes and reached for a brush. Gently stroking her hair, she coaxed out the tangles and pushed the shining folds into place.

With one last glance in the mirror, she stepped back into the other room and stood for a moment, uncertain where to proceed next. Seeing the window, she walked up to it and drew back the curtain to check the weather. The sight that met her made her gasp in delight.

Gillian's cabin was set against a little patch of trees with a clearing in front of it. A path led to the right where she supposed the rest of the camp was, but on the other side there was the gentle slope of grass overlooking a beautiful clear blue lake. Beyond the lake was the most incredible sight of all. Huge, rugged cliffs of an enormous mountain towered around her. Below, trees surrounded the lake, lending a peaceful atmosphere, which seemed in sharp contrast to the rocky crevices of the bare, menacing mountain.

She remembered many of the photographs others had shown her, but none could compare with the wonder before her now. It took Gillian a moment to drink in the scene, but soon she dropped the curtain and ran outside to stand beside the lake.

The water near her feet lapped against scattered rocks, but Gillian could see that it was not this way all around the lake. Elsewhere the trees ran all the way down to the water's edge and several bent precariously out over the lake. Rough vegetation mixed with the sturdy evergreens and Poplar to form a thick forest, but the lake itself was as clear and clean as she had ever imagined a lake could be.

The reflection of the mountain lay shimmering on the lake. If she could not see the real fortress towering before her, she would find it easy to believe the water's shifting surface was only a mirage created by the wind as it danced across the lake.

Slowly, Gillian felt herself begin to move along the water's edge, allowing her feet to carry her wherever they chose. She continued until the beach turned into the forest and still she walked on. Soon she saw a large twisted tree bending down close to the water. She felt compelled to climb out onto it. It was not as easy to do as she had imagined, but soon she had maneuvered out onto the large trunk.

When she had come to rest, she drew in a deep breath

and let her eyes wander up the mountainside, over its peaks and into the clouds, then fall peacefully back down to the far shore of the lake and rest on the grassy softness of a meadow far to her left. At last she pulled her vision back to the water lapping slowly beneath her, looking deep into its shadowy depths.

Suddenly her focus snapped onto the surface of the water slightly to her left as the form of another person appeared. Gillian's head jerked up to look behind her at the man standing on the shore by the base of her tree. An uncontrolled gasp left her throat.

"Pardon me," the deep voice apologized. "I didn't mean to startle you. I couldn't bring myself to take you away from your revelry."

"No," Gillian replied quickly, "you don't need to apologize. I shouldn't have been startled, but it's just so incredible here and I couldn't think of anything else." She paused for a moment, looking around and then adding with a deep blush, "That sounds awfully silly, doesn't it?"

"Not at all," the man said with an understanding smile. "I find myself doing the same thing. There's nothing else in the world that can compare to the sight of Mount Judas in the morning."

"Is that its name?" Gillian mused. "Why do they call it that?"

"In the winter, storms from it can be as treacherous and unpredictable as Judas ever was."

It was not until then that Gillian really noticed the man before her. He was tall, with a full build, perhaps in his early sixties, with graying hair and a very wise-looking, weathered face. He appeared out of place in his rough blue jeans, like a polished executive in sneakers; but his sensitive brown eyes looked as if they could really sparkle with fun.

Slowly and carefully, Gillian climbed back onto the bank and stood looking up at the stranger.

"My name is Gillian Todd," she said cordially, extending her hand, startled by her sudden boldness.

"And my name is Jacob Winters," the man replied, giving her hand a firm shake, and then added with a flicker of a smile, "but please, call me Jake. Everyone does."

"Jake," Gillian responded, testing the sound of it. "I'm not certain where I'm supposed to be right now. I just started to work for this camp, and I haven't been told what to do today. Could you please tell me where to find Kate Phillips?"

"It just so happens that Kate told me to find you and show you around the camp. I'm supposed to leave you at the kitchen when I'm done. She'll meet you there. Is that all right with you?"

"Okay," Gillian answered cheerfully, but cast a last longing look over her shoulder at the lake. She was determined to spend as much time as possible in this enchanting place. Part of her longed to stay there, while the other could hardly wait to see the rest of the camp.

"Then let's get going," Jake said, smiling back, and the two set off to acquaint Gillian with the rest of her new surroundings.

———

Jake took Gillian down the path that led past her cabin to where the center of activity was. The camp itself was set up like a wagon wheel. Gillian's cabin was down one of the spokes that pointed out all around its hub. At the hub itself were three large buildings. The first held the dining area and kitchen. Jake passed it, saying that it would be the last stop on their tour.

The next building was the lodge. It was a large two-story, octagonal building with roughly finished wooden walls and a high, pointed roof.

Jake led the way to a set of glass doors that opened into

a lounge. The room had a large, sunken firepit in the center with benches built around it. Full-length windows filled the room with light, and flourishing plants stood in front of them.

"Why don't we step into the main office and see if Terry is there? She's the camp receptionist and bookkeeper. I think she has some papers for you to sign. It shouldn't take too long."

Jake led Gillian through the lounge to a row of doors lining the other side of it. Above the doors, a balcony looked over the room. Gillian couldn't help noticing its elegance.

"What is the second floor used for?" Gillian inquired.

"It has several rooms for any of the guests who prefer not to stay in a cabin," he answered and then knocked on the closest door.

Gillian made a mental note. This is where she would be staying.

"Come in," a muffled voice called from inside, and Jake held the door while Gillian entered.

"Terry, this is Gillian Todd. She's come to take Wayne Corvey's place in the kitchen. Kate said you might have some forms for her to sign."

"Yes," Terry answered quickly and flipped through a stack of papers on her desk. Turning to Gillian, she explained, "These are the basic forms. It won't take you more than a couple of minutes to complete them."

Gillian was handed a pen and shown to a small table where she began the tedious work of filling out the forms. She had forgotten that this would be part of her orientation.

Jake and Terry chatted while Gillian completed the paperwork. Terry then took the forms and welcomed her to the camp.

"Are you ready to see some more?" Jake asked as they returned to the lounge.

"Let's go," Gillian answered enthusiastically, and they set out again.

The next building held the central restrooms, showers, and laundry facilities. Gillian stored this information away. She was sure a shower would be relaxing after this busy day was over—even if it was a long way to walk from her cabin. Perhaps when she moved into the lodge there would be showers in each of the rooms—or at least just down the hall.

Turning back to the way they had come, Jake showed Gillian down the trail to the right of the one leading to her cabin. This trail led to the opposite side of the lake she had seen earlier. Gillian noted several other cabins in this area. These were available for the campers, Jake told her.

The cluster of cabins looked deserted, and Gillian tried to picture what they would be like when they were filled with fishermen and hunters. She mentally counted the number of people she would be serving. It seemed like a lot of responsibility.

Gillian thought about this as she walked back down the path toward the hub of the camp. It wasn't until then that she realized her job was very important. For the first time she questioned whether she would be able to operate the large kitchen. The manager before her had succeeded, she had heard, and that fact seemed to put even more pressure on her. She would always be compared with the previous manager—perhaps not out loud, but at least in the minds of those around her. Could she stand up to this test? She wasn't sure, but she knew that she wanted to try.

Jake had noticed that Gillian was deep in thought, so he had not disturbed her. Now they were moving down the next path, away from the camp again, and he drew her attention back to the tour.

"These are the stables," Jake was saying.

"Oh!" cried Gillian, leaving her deep thoughts, "I hadn't realized there would be horses."

"I'm afraid I can't give you much help here. It's not my department. When I was younger I rode some, but it doesn't feel quite the same anymore," Jake admitted humbly.

"Now, Jake," a voice drawled from nowhere, "that's just an excuse. You're the kind that gets younger every day." In a moment, a tall man followed the voice out of the building in front of them, chuckling as he came. The man, though slightly hunched over, walked with a deliberate swagger. Gillian thought he was the perfect image of a western cowboy.

"Randy," Jake said good-naturedly, "this is Gillian Todd. She came to manage the kitchen."

"Hi," Gillian returned and then bubbled, forgetting to feel nervous about talking to a stranger. "It must be exciting to take care of horses all day. I love to ride." Then she blushed a deep red. "That is," she added, "I love horses. Actually, I've never ridden one in my life."

"I could saddle up one of these mangy critters right now if you had a mind to take a riding lesson. What do you say?"

"I don't think so," Gillian stammered, suddenly realizing how ridiculous she must have sounded.

"You don't have to prove anything," Jake responded, coming to her rescue. "You've got all the time in the world, and don't let Randy here try to pressure you into anything you're not ready for."

Jake quickly stole Randy's attention away from Gillian's plight, and the two men talked for a moment about some future event the camp was planning. While they stood talking behind her, Gillian walked forward and stood at the door of the stable. In reality, Gillian had seen a horse only from a distance. They had always held a fascination for her, but she had never had a chance to face one. Now here was an opportunity to climb onto the back of an animal larger than herself, and she was filled with fear at the thought.

Slowly and quietly Gillian crept forward and glanced into the first stall. It was dark inside the barn, but as her eyes grew accustomed to the dimness, she perceived a huddled form lying on the floor at the front of the stall. Cautiously, she stepped closer and bent over the top rail to get a better look. The form began to take shape, and slowly she realized it was a tiny foal. The little colt fluttered one leg out in front of it and rocked forward in an effort to stand. Its feeble legs were unable to hold it and it toppled down again.

A smile of delight played across Gillian's face as she watched the little fellow. She forgot the men outside and the rest of her surroundings and was totally caught up in the struggles of the baby in front of her. She was so involved that she did not notice the mare walk forward from the corner far to her left until she was directly at Gillian's elbow.

Suddenly Gillian was aware of breath on her hand and she jumped back in surprise. The mare, startled by the sudden movement, also swung her head violently upward. To Gillian, this movement was aggressive, and as she looked into the mare's eyes she was certain she saw an angry glare. Before she was able to think, Gillian whirled out the door and away from what she imagined to be the raving animal following her.

Randy howled with laughter when he saw Gillian flee from the barn. He knew that the only animals kept there presently were the gentle mare and her innocent little colt, born late the night before.

"Another greenhorn!" he hooted to Jake. "This could be lots of fun."

Seeing that she was the cause of Randy's amusement, Gillian came back to her senses. A deep red blush spread across her face, and her pulse quickened.

"Maybe I should show you the rest of the camp," Jake suggested quickly.

"I'd like that," Gillian muttered, staring down the path

directly in front of her while they walked away. Randy was still laughing heartily behind her.

The next spoke of the wheel was the road by which Gillian had entered the camp the night before, so Jake led her past it to the next path. This one led down to the practice range where the hunters could spend an afternoon brushing up on their riflery skills. Some daring souls even tried their hand at archery, but, Gillian noticed, those targets were not generally worn in the middle of the bull's-eye.

From there Jake took Gillian on a shortcut through a wooded area to the boating docks. Here the icy water formed a quiet little inlet, with the shore falling steeply to the bottom of the lake. Seeing four motor boats and some canoes tied to the docks, Gillian found herself wondering if she might not like to try boating sometime. The rugged atmosphere seemed to be drawing her already.

On the way back to camp, Jake explained that the small lake on which Gillian's cabin sat was not used for boating and fishing. It was connected to this larger one by a narrow stream.

At last Gillian and Jake were back at the hub. They had made a complete circle and then stopped in the shade of one of the large trees to rest.

"There seems to be so much to do here," Gillian remarked thoughtfully. "How can the camp employ enough people to take care of everything?"

"Well," Jake said smiling, "God has been good to us. You would be surprised at how much it is worth to some men to spend a weekend in the mountains. Often, the men who stay with us want the sense of being on their own. That is why we don't supervise the boating docks and the riflery range on a regular basis. It gives them a feeling of roughing it."

"Where do the staff live?" Gillian prodded further.

Jake smiled again. "I thought you would have seen their

cabins this morning. They are in the forest around your cabin. Some are back quite far because it's really quiet in the woods. By the time the workers have put in a long day, they want to spend the evening hours as peacefully as possible."

Don't any of them stay in the lodge? Gillian thought to herself.

"How would you like to see your office now?" Jake suggested.

"Okay. I am getting pretty curious to see it."

"Then follow me."

4

$\mathcal{J}$ake walked to the door of the dining hall and opened it with great ceremony while Gillian peered cautiously inside. The room was deserted since the camp was temporarily closed. It looked abandoned and eerie, with chairs turned up on the tables where they had been left after the room had been cleaned.

To her right were two serving tables. Behind these was a large window leading into the kitchen with doors on either side through which the serving was done.

On the opposite side of the dining room was a large stone fireplace, adding a comfortable feeling to the room. On the wall across from Gillian was another door leading outside and, to the right of it, yet another large window into the kitchen which Gillian assumed was used by the diners to dispose of their used dishes as they left the room.

As she looked around the room, Gillian walked slowly forward so that by the time she had noticed the dish disposal, she was directly in front of the serving tables.

"Why don't you just go on into the kitchen?" Jake called after her, "I'll call Kate and then meet you back there in a couple of minutes."

Still in awe of everything she'd seen, Gillian pushed through one of the doors without replying and entered the kitchen.

It was a spotless room filled with stainless steel tables and equipment. Neat racks of utensils and pots hung here and there with rows of dishes in open cupboards.

It was easy to tell that the left-hand side of the kitchen was used to wash the dishes. The window she had supposed to be a dish disposal opened to a double sink with two spray hoses. The dishes would be rinsed and then loaded onto trays to be put through the dishwashing machine. When they came out on the other side, they would be unloaded and set in their storage places throughout the rest of the kitchen. There was also a separate sink for scrubbing pots and pans.

On the other side of the kitchen were the cooking sections. There were three ovens, a large grill, several tables for food preparation, and a large door opening into a cooler.

It was just after Gillian had inspected the cooler that Jake walked in.

"What do you think?" Jake asked.

"It's bigger than I imagined," Gillian replied slowly. "I have never worked in a kitchen this large."

"I guess you'd better get used to it," he grinned.

"How many people do you suppose are served here at one meal?"

"Not more than a couple dozen, usually. At certain peak times during the year we get up to fifty, so we have to make the facilities big enough to handle that many."

"That'll be enough to keep me busy," Gillian commented with a nervous laugh.

"They do expect good food, though. That's the tough part. These men are all quite well off and they want to be treated accordingly," Jake explained seriously. "Sometimes some of them can be pretty demanding."

Gillian felt a little apprehensive at the thought.

"I was told there would be several other employees in the kitchen who have worked here for some time, and that they might, well, help me get started. I learned a lot about managing during college, but it might take me a while to get really good at it. I mean, I *think* I can do it, but . . . well, I'll do my best."

"Of course," Jake assured her, placing his rough hand encouragingly on her shoulder. "You'll do just fine. And we'll *all* help you any way we can." Just then Kate entered.

"Good morning, Gillian. What do you think of the camp so far?"

"This place is beautiful!" she answered sincerely.

"Well, I hope you'll soon feel at home. Do you want something to eat before we start whipping this kitchen into shape?" she asked, already reaching for plates and glasses.

"That sounds great," Gillian replied, realizing how hungry she was.

The day went very quickly. Gillian found it easy to listen to Kate's jabber while they worked, and was pleased that they got along so well. The kitchen soon took shape and Gillian was able to feel as if it really was her domain.

Although Gillian had worried at first that Kate would take over, Kate made a sincere effort to help Gillian feel in charge. Each time there was a decision to be made, she would offer a suggestion and then look to Gillian for a final answer. On a couple of occasions, Gillian questioned Kate, but it was never a problem. Kate simply accepted her judgment, and the two kept working together without a hitch.

Near the end of the afternoon, Kate showed Gillian to an office in the back and explained that it would be hers. She could use anything that was already there and, if there was anything else she felt she needed, all she had to do was ask.

The two women then sat down while Kate explained the budget for the kitchen. Afterward she asked Gillian how soon she thought the kitchen could be put into use.

Gillian knew there was still a great deal of work to be done before everything would be in working order. The cooler needed to be restocked and new menus planned. The help had to be assigned specific duties and a work schedule drawn up. As Gillian sat listing all that needed to be done, she realized she was doing exactly what she had learned in a course for restaurant management. She was excited and eager to begin using the knowledge she had gained. How glad she was that she hadn't taken the job at the flower shop! The satisfaction she felt now had certainly been worth the long trip.

At last Gillian decided she could be ready by the following Monday morning.

"Are you sure you want to push yourself?" Kate asked cautiously. "That gives you less than a week."

"I know it will take some work, but I'm sure I can have things in order by then."

"All right, Gillian. Monday it is."

The two ate a quick supper that Kate prepared, explaining that Gillian would be doing plenty of kitchen work soon enough.

After supper, Kate excused herself to attend a meeting with Terry, and Gillian walked back to her cabin, deep in thought.

There was still a lot to do in the kitchen before Monday. Gillian wondered if she would be ready in time.

Suddenly she remembered that she hadn't told Kate about her intended move to the lodge. Well, one more night in the cabin wouldn't be so bad. It really was cozy, even if it didn't offer all the modern conveniences Gillian was used to.

As she walked, she watched carefully for any sign of another cabin near her. For quite some time she didn't see anything, but finally there was a noise off to the right of the path.

Curiosity got the best of her, and she started off in search of the source. Gillian did not walk far before she came to a tiny cabin tucked away in a small clearing.

It was a beautiful location with a little stream trickling

beside it, its mossy banks lined with tiny wild flowers.

Gillian walked up to the cabin and then lost her nerve, feeling she was intruding on its occupant. Just as she turned to leave, the door opened and a pan of water splashed out onto the ground, far too close to where she was standing. With a little gasp, Gillian dodged the water. At the sudden motion, a head poked out the door to see what had happened.

"Sorry!" a tall young man with a heavy British-sounding accent exclaimed. "I had no idea anyone was around."

"It's my fault," Gillian blushed. "I shouldn't have gone sneaking up to your cabin unannounced."

"Well, since you're here," the man continued good-naturedly, stepping out onto the low cement porch of his cabin and smiling down at Gillian, "why don't you introduce yourself?"

"My name's Gillian Todd," she said, still blushing deeply. "I'm going to be the new kitchen manager."

"That's a lot of work you've taken on. Do you think you can manage? You seem terribly young for something of that caliber."

The statement made Gillian feel slightly perturbed. She hadn't noticed the teasing twinkle in his eye and the playful flicker of a dimple on his cheek.

"I have a degree in hotel and restaurant management," she answered firmly. "I'm sure I can handle it."

"Oh, if you've studied it, then I'm certain you will."

The conversation seemed to stop and Gillian looked anxiously around for a chance to leave the uncomfortable situation.

"Why don't you come in for a while," the man spoke up amiably, catching her off guard.

"I—" Gillian tried to think quickly. "I really should be getting back to my cabin. I've got a lot to do," she finished lamely.

"Wayne, the previous manager, didn't seem to find many ways to manage the kitchen from his cabin. Perhaps you've been taught some new technique." The man tried to look very serious, but his blue-gray eyes danced with laughter.

"I need to organize."

"Organize what?"

"Oh," Gillian replied, feeling distraught at this point, "it's just some things that need to be taken care of. You probably wouldn't be interested at all."

"Why don't you let *me* decide. Perhaps I could help you," he continued, and from the twinkle in his eyes and the flicker of his blond mustache, Gillian was convinced that the whole situation amused him greatly.

"No, thank you," Gillian stammered in an effort to sound final. "I have to work it out alone. Goodbye."

"Goodbye for now, then," he called, but she was already trudging through the trees away from his cabin.

The nerve of that man! Gillian muttered inwardly as she stomped down the path. *He had a really wonderful time making a fool out of me. Well, I'm nobody's fool! That kitchen will be ready by Monday if for no other reason than to make him see I'm not a silly little girl.*

Gillian did spend the evening sorting and planning for the days ahead. By the time she crawled into bed, she had a very good idea of what needed to be done and on which day it could best be accomplished. Though she had stayed up late and was very tired, somehow as she lay under the thick quilt, she could not make herself fall asleep. Her mind kept wandering to the annoying man. He had made her so angry.

Imagine, she thought to herself, *a man being so rude to someone he's never even met before. In all my life I've never met anyone who made me feel so stupid. And he did it on purpose, too. I surely hope our paths don't have to cross very often. The nerve of him!* She rolled over as if to go to sleep. However, sleep was an elusive thing that night. For a long time, Gillian tossed and turned, seeing the blue-gray eyes dancing before her in the dark and the teasing smile curled up under the blond mustache.

5

*T*he next morning Gillian woke with a will to master the day. Her mind buzzed with what needed to be accomplished, and she hurried through her morning preparations in order to get it all done.

As she hustled along the path to the showers, her travel bag packed with clean clothes and other necessary supplies, she saw Jake. He was walking down the path in front of her, whistling a merry tune to the beautiful morning.

"Jake," Gillian called out to him.

"Good morning, Gillian," Jake responded as he stopped to wait for her to catch up.

"And how are you this fine morning?" Jake asked with an enthusiastic smile.

"Wonderful," Gillian replied with equal radiance. "I'm all set to get a lot accomplished today."

"Good for you," Jake answered, and the two set off together down the path toward the center of camp, chatting amiably.

After Gillian had showered and blown her hair dry, she hurried to the kitchen to begin her organizing. Today she planned to take an inventory of the supplies on hand and to make a list of anything else she would need. This meant she would have to make up the menus for the next week so that she'd be sure to have all the necessary items.

In order to do this, she would have to search through the recipes used most frequently and pick some for the next week. There was no sense trying to find new recipes since she had no idea what kind of quantities she would need.

When she reached the kitchen, she ate a quick breakfast and began to look through the recipe file. Soon, she was plunged deeply into her work, stopping only for a light snack midafternoon.

The day went so quickly that when Gillian was finished, she discovered it was getting dark outside. She had not realized it was that late. So after quickly putting things back into place, she wandered out into the evening air on her way back to her cabin.

As she looked around her, she saw a light in the lodge. Curious, she wandered over to it and was surprised to hear singing coming from inside.

Gillian could not resist the urge to peek in the door and was surprised to see a number of people, whom she supposed to be staff members, sitting and singing together. Singing had never been a big part of her life, and she wasn't used to seeing other people sitting around singing enthusiastically.

Suddenly the music stopped and Gillian heard a familiar voice begin to speak. It did not take her long to realize it was Jake.

This was too much for Gillian's curiosity, so, assuring herself that no one would mind, she crept quietly into the lodge and sat down on a chair near the back. Jake saw her and smiled, but kept talking. He spoke of camp opening again soon and the responsibility it placed on all of the staff.

Gillian assumed it was some kind of pep talk and settled back to listen halfheartedly.

"We must all take a moment to reevaluate our importance here," Jake was saying. "God has placed us in this camp as a ministry."

That's a strange way to put it, Gillian thought to herself.

"We are all His servants," Jake continued. "God put us here for a purpose.

"Now, we all believe that God calls pastors and missionaries, but what about camp counselors, wranglers, grounds keepers, and kitchen help? Doesn't God also have a service for them to do?

"In 1 Corinthians 12, we see that each of the members of the body is important. We can't all be one of the directors, but that doesn't mean we are any less important. We need each other.

"Certainly, this leaves us with a responsibility to do whatever work is assigned to us in the best way we can.

"In 1 Peter 4:11 we read this, 'If anyone speaks, he should do it as one speaking the very words of God. If anyone serves, he should do it with the strength God provides, so that in all things God may be praised through Jesus Christ.'

"In this verse we see that God intends for us to do our best at whatever service He has given us. We need to take these words seriously. He hasn't just put us here in order to get us out of the way." The sound of stifled chuckling rose across the gathering. "He really needs us to fill our spot and accomplish what He has planned for our lives."

Jake kept talking, but Gillian found her thoughts beginning to wander. *Why is Jake saying so much about God? Is he "religious"?* The idea scared her somewhat. She had often heard her friends talk about religious fanatics. But when she remembered her morning with him, she knew he had not acted unusual. He was one of the most considerate people she had met and she had felt comfortable with him immediately.

What was he doing, then? Suppose he was religious. She had known a few people who claimed they were religious, yet it hadn't made any difference in their lives. They

were just like anyone else. The only difference was their be-
lief in God.

Maybe that was why Jake was saying those things. He
believed there was a God or something.

Gillian believed that there was a God, too, she supposed. Maybe Jake and she were not so different. Jake was
just willing to talk about God.

When the meeting was over, Gillian rose quickly to
leave before anyone noticed she had been there, but Jake
hurried back toward her, calling her name.

"I'm so glad you came," he said when he had reached
her side. "I was supposed to ask you this morning to come,
but it completely slipped my mind at that time."

"That's okay," Gillian assured him. "I heard the singing
and my curiosity took over. Dad says my curiosity works
overtime."

"I'm glad you came," Jake continued. "I was watching
for you. Say, how would you like a companion on the walk
home?"

"That would be nice," Gillian smiled.

"Okay. I'll be with you just as soon as I can gather my
things."

Jake left and Gillian waited outside by the door. As the
people came out of the building, they noticed her standing
there. Some smiled, others said "hi," and still others introduced themselves and chatted with her for a moment.

Jake was soon back and the two walked off toward their
cabins. It was a cool night and the stars were twinkling so
clearly in the sky that they seemed close enough to touch.
Once again Gillian was amazed at how beautiful her new
surroundings were, and her gaze settled on the mountains
that pushed against the sky, seeming to hold it in place.

"You like it here, don't you?" Jake stated quietly.

"Yes, I do," Gillian responded. "It's so peaceful and se-
rene. I could stay out here all night and never get tired of

looking at the stars. Do you know any of the constellations, Jake?"

"Not many, I'm afraid. Just the two dippers and the North Star."

"Where are they?" Gillian prodded.

The two stopped and Jake pointed out the constellations. It was difficult for Gillian to see them at first, but Jake was patient and she finally recognized the Big Dipper.

"Jake," she asked slowly, not knowing how to phrase her question, "About your talk tonight—do you really think we need to serve God? I mean, isn't He too busy to notice us?"

Jake paused for a moment and then spoke up softly. "I believe God created the world and is the One who is keeping it in order. But I also believe He loves and cares for each person who is alive now, who lived before us, and who will be born in the future."

"Why would He care for me? I've never done anything that would make Him love me."

"That's the wonder of it," Jake smiled knowingly. "If we had to do something to make Him love us, we might as well give up. I don't understand either, but for some reason He loves us as His children."

"In a way, that sounds wonderful," Gillian said thoughtfully, "but in a way it scares me, too. If He's watching everything I do like religious people say He is, I'm embarrassed. I don't think I want Him seeing some of the things I do."

"We all feel that way sometimes, Gillian. The wonderful thing is He is willing, and even waiting, to forgive us for all of those kinds of things. Nothing would make Him happier than to release us from them."

Wait a minute, Gillian thought, *who said that I was sorry? I just said that I'd be embarrassed, and that's all. I wouldn't give up all of life's pleasures that easily.*

Out loud she answered, "That sounds nice. I guess it would make some people feel better to say 'God, forgive me,' but I can't see that it would make any real difference."

Jake drew in a quiet breath. Realizing she wasn't open to any more discussion, he quickly changed the subject to lighter matters and they continued toward their cabins.

Again, Gillian slept fitfully. This time her mind seemed to be fighting within itself, as though against an unwanted intruder.

Why does what Jake said bother me so much? she kept thinking. *I've never thought much about God before. So why now? I don't need to be forgiven and I'm not really sorry, either. What I do doesn't hurt God at all, so why should He expect an apology? But if I'm not sorry, then why do I suddenly feel so guilty? It's Jake's fault,* she concluded. *He's the one who got me started thinking about this. And since it's only Jake making me feel guilty, then I should be able to just push it aside.* But the more Gillian tried to blame Jake, the more she realized it wasn't him at all.

The next morning finally arrived, and Gillian struggled from her fitful sleep. Even her shower didn't do much to raise her spirits, though she tried desperately to wash away the gloom. When she arrived at the kitchen, Kate met her and asked if she was ready to ride into town.

"I could be in about an hour," Gillian answered.

"Okay. I'll tell Kyle to pick you up right outside. He'll take you into town and Jake will meet you there to bring you back. How long do you think you'll need to make the kitchen purchases?"

"Not more than a couple of hours."

"I'll tell Jake to pick you up at noon, then. It takes a good three quarters of an hour to drive to Cedarview, and that should give you lots of time to shop. Just charge your purchases at the store. They're used to us doing that."

"Thanks, Kate," Gillian said, trying to smile without yawning.

When Kate was gone, Gillian set to work getting her list from the office and making a few refinements. In a short time she heard the sound of a car horn and hurried to the door.

The sight that met her made her heart skip a beat. Before her, moving to open the car door, was the obnoxious man with the laughing eyes and the evil grin. But Kate had said that someone named Kyle would be driving her into town. This had to be him. She hadn't asked the man's name when they first met.

"Come, come, now," he grinned. "Let's not take all day."

Gillian moved stiffly toward the car and into the passenger's seat. She winced when she realized Kate had said the trip would take a good three quarters of an hour. It would seem like an eternity.

Kyle crawled in under the steering wheel and said playfully, "G'day. Welcome to Kyle's taxi service. Where to, ma'am?"

Gillian stifled a groan and shrank down into her seat.

The car pulled out of the driveway and started down the road to the gate.

"I believe I owe you an apology," Kyle said unexpectedly, making Gillian blink twice. "I shouldn't have had such sport with you the other day. I am sorry if I offended you."

His accent emphasized his playful manner, and Gillian had to scrutinize him carefully to decide whether or not he was teasing again. His mustache wasn't quivering in laughter, and his eyes seemed almost serious, so she assumed he meant what he said.

"It's all right," Gillian weakened. "I guess I was out of place to come barging in on you unannounced."

"Oh, but you didn't barge in at all," Kyle responded.

"You were only looking for companionship and I greeted you with a panful of water. It's I who should be remorseful."

It was all that Gillian could do to hold back a giggle. "Where are you from?" Gillian asked quickly to cover her mirth.

"I'm from Calgary," Kyle answered. "Where are you from?"

"I mean," Gillian began again, embarrassed by her awkward question, "where did you get your accent? Are you British?"

"A common misconception," Kyle answered, unaffected. "Actually, I'm Australian. The accent is close to British but not quite the same."

"How long have you been in Canada?"

"For only two years. I came across to visit a sickly aunt and never left. I stayed for a year, intending to move back to Australia, but it never happened. After a year I gave up deceiving myself and became a Canadian citizen. I want to return to Australia for a visit someday, but Canada is my home now. You haven't answered my question, though. Where are *you* from?"

Still feeling like a nervous schoolgirl in Kyle's presence, Gillian answered, "I'm from the U.S. I lived in a small city in the Midwest. It was a nice place to grow up and I thought I'd never leave, but—well, it's nice here, too. And the countryside back home doesn't even begin to compare with this." Gillian finished looking around her, surprised at how deeply she felt about the area already.

"Yes, the Rockies are truly magnificent," Kyle agreed. "Do you think you'll stay?"

"Oh no, I don't think so." Gillian's mind turned back to her promise to leave after one year. Kyle mustn't think she was planning to stay, but she didn't want him to know she was planning to leave either. "But I know wherever I live I'll think about this place often," she finished lamely.

"That's the first step, you know," Kyle grinned. "Once you let this mountain air affect you, you're never quite the same."

The conversation came to a lull and for a while Gillian watched the scenery fly past her, thinking about his words and fidgeting with the strap of her purse.

Suddenly Kyle called out, "Look there. Do you see that doe and her fawn?"

Gillian scanned the side of the road and exclaimed, "Kyle, they're so still. They don't even flinch."

Just as the car came close to them, the deer turned away and, in a single move, bounded into the thick growth beside the road. Gillian sat looking after them but they were gone from sight.

"Do you see wild animals like that very often?" she asked breathlessly.

"Quite often, in fact," Kyle answered with a hint of pride. "It is a common thing to see deer, bears, and all kinds of animals by the roadside."

"Bears!" Gillian gasped. "Do they come very close to camp?"

"At times," Kyle laughed. "The trick is not to be around when they do."

This thought stole some of Gillian's delight. A bear was not something she would choose to meet anywhere. She thought back over all the times she had walked down the path to her cabin alone. If she had seen a bear on that path, she couldn't imagine what she would have done.

"There really is nothing to worry about," Kyle interrupted her thoughts. "If you don't bother the bears and are careful not to tempt them by leaving food scraps around, they'll leave you alone." This statement did little to make her feel safe.

Before long the car drove through Linden. Gillian remembered arriving on the bus in this small town. In the daylight the town looked even more empty, and it seemed that the wilderness was closing in on every side. Main street was the only street she could see.

The remainder of the ride went without incident or conversation. It seemed forever until Gillian found herself being assisted out of the car.

"Thank you very much for the ride, Kyle," she offered with sincerity, not daring to look at him directly.

"Think nothing of it," Kyle answered. "I had business in town anyway. Have a good day," and in a moment he was gone.

Business in town anyway, Gillian echoed in her mind, and then the practical side of her reprimanded, *Of course, he did. Do you really think he made the long trip just to ride with you?* With that conclusion her spirit was a little less buoyant as she turned to look around.

It did not take Gillian long to find the grocery store. The next two hours were spent comparing prices and testing the quality of the produce. Gillian was again amazed at how much help her education was to her. She knew just what to look for in the produce section and how to get the best meat value.

When she finished her shopping, she sat outside with her three loaded shopping carts to wait for Jake. It was not long until she was once again in a car, this time heading back toward camp.

6

*T*he remainder of the week was constantly busy for Gillian. She met all of the kitchen staff and assigned the new work schedule. For the most part, she was excited about Monday, but she had some fears, too, as she looked to the day.

Kate had commented on how smoothly Gillian had gotten the kitchen into working order, but she still faced the real test. Could she properly oversee the preparation of a meal?

Monday's breakfast went very smoothly because few campers had arrived. As the morning wore on, Gillian stole several glances out the window and began to feel nervous. Through her eyes it seemed that there were hundreds of people outside.

Kate was to stop by at eleven o'clock to give her an estimate of how many people she would be serving. The thought was somewhat comforting, but she was still haunted by all the terrible catastrophes that could occur.

The staff arrived on time and the serving tables were set up. Everything seemed to be going according to plan. At twelve o'clock, just as Gillian had set the last of the serving dishes on the line, Tim, one of the kitchen helpers, threw open the dining room doors to signal the beginning of the noon meal.

A line of people formed at each side of the serving table, and men of various sizes and shapes began filing past.

Most served themselves and went to sit down without comment, but several mentioned how good the food looked.

Gillian smiled to herself. Maybe there would be no problems at all. Maybe she had worried for nothing.

"Hey, lady," a voice broke into her thoughts, "what does a guy have to do to get served around here?"

Gillian looked up quickly, startled by the comment. There before her stood Randy. "A man has to humble himself and do his own serving," Gillian laughed back. Even Randy could not annoy her on this day.

Randy laughed and began to help himself. Just before he left he tossed over his shoulder, "Not bad, cookie."

From that point on, Gillian did not walk, she floated. Randy's comment had made her feel that she could stop worrying and enjoy herself.

By the time the meal was over, Gillian felt as though she deserved to be in control. She instructed her workers to clear the tables and put things back in order. Then, because she was still so pleased with herself, she impulsively dismissed them and washed up the pots and pans herself. No one complained.

After the cleaning up was done, Gillian found herself with time to spare before the next meal. She left a list of directions for the kitchen staff about the next meal and walked slowly back in the direction of her cabin. When she arrived, she allowed herself the pleasure of taking a long walk around the lake. She took off her shoes and socks and waded in the cool water, humming cheerfully.

The afternoon went quickly and before Gillian had had enough of the revelry, she realized she should be getting back to the kitchen to oversee the preparation of the next meal.

She walked slowly back to her cabin to freshen up and then headed toward the kitchen.

Dinner went as smoothly as lunch, even though there

were a few more campers and it was a more elaborate meal. Everyone made positive comments about the food and Gillian passed these along to her staff before she released them after the meal was cleaned away.

"Just a minute, Gillian," Sharon, one of the cooks, called after her as she headed to her office for one last check of the plans for the next day. "Are you going to vespers tonight?"

"What's 'vespers'?" Gillian asked.

"You were there last week. It's the meeting we have every Monday and Wednesday in the lodge at eight o'clock."

Gillian remembered the meeting where she had heard Jake speak the week before. "I don't think so," she answered. "I have work to do."

"Well, if you can make it," Sharon continued, "I'd sure like to go with you." Her warm brown eyes were smiling as usual.

Gillian smiled back, feeling somewhat awkward about what to say next. They didn't know each other very well. What if she told Sharon that she simply wasn't interested in the meeting? Would Sharon be hurt, or worse yet, think less of Gillian because of it?

"I'll see you tomorrow," Gillian muttered to break the silence, pretending to be quite busy. When she realized how much her statement sounded like a dismissal, she winced.

"Sure," Sharon answered evenly and walked out into the cool evening air.

Why did I do that? Gillian scolded herself. *I get so nervous about what to say that I say something stupid. Sharon was just trying to be friendly and I was so rude. Someday I've got to learn how to relax when I talk to someone I don't know very well.*

———

The week went by very quickly and on Thursday night Gillian found herself reflecting over her days at the camp while she wrote letters to her parents and to Krystal. There had been many good things about it and few problems.

Jake was a wonderful man. He was quite a few years older than Gillian, but she enjoyed his company a great deal. He had almost become a father figure to her, yet no one could match her dad. She thought of Jake as more of a lovable uncle.

Sharon was a lot of fun to work with and went out of her way to help. Gillian really enjoyed her company. Yet, there was still something that held them apart. To Gillian, it seemed that the invisible barrier she often put up between herself and those she didn't know well was once again standing firmly between her and a would-be friend.

Randy stopped by the kitchen quite often to plague her about taking riding lessons. *Just like a pesky brother,* Gillian thought. She appreciated his friendliness and had even begun to enjoy his jokes. Saturday she had squirted him with the spray hose when he'd offered to help her wash a few pots. He took a joke almost as well as he gave it—but not quite.

Gillian did not see much of Kate, but when she did it was always enjoyable. However, she always thought of her as more of a boss than a companion even though Kate seemed to be doing her best to reverse the order.

Kyle was not around very often, but when Gillian did get a chance to chat with him, she liked it very much. He was becoming easier to talk with, and she found herself looking forward to seeing him again. She still blushed when she thought of their first encounter and how badly she had misjudged his intentions.

Friday after lunch, Randy showed up and insisted that Gillian come down to the stables to at least pet the horses even if she did not plan to ride one.

"All right, I'll come," she replied reluctantly, "but if you laugh at me again, I'll walk away and not look back."

"I promise not to laugh," Randy grinned, leading the way to the stables.

By the time they arrived, Randy had talked Gillian into trying to ride the gentle mare that had frightened her so badly the week before. It did not take him long to saddle the horse and lead her out to where Gillian was standing.

"May I introduce Miss Polly," Randy said with a bow toward Gillian. "Miss Polly, this is Gillian."

"Good afternoon, Miss Polly," Gillian said, going along with the game.

"Miss Polly," Randy continued, "Gillian would like the honor of riding you. Would you mind?"

Just at that moment, the horse sneezed and Randy laughed, saying that Miss Polly had given her approval.

The mare stood very still while Gillian climbed into the saddle in a rather ungraceful way. When Randy handed her the reins, she suddenly felt her stomach sink.

"Now all you do is nudge her with your heel if you want her to move. If you want to go right, you lay the rein on the left against the left side of her neck. It's opposite if you want to go left. Simple enough, right?"

"How do I make her stop?" Gillian asked soberly.

"Just pull back gently on the reins."

Gillian thought for a moment and then decided to try the command to turn before she actually started to move. She pulled the reins to the left as Randy had instructed her and laid the right rein against Miss Polly's neck.

Without warning the mare began to move. Gillian was so startled that she almost slipped out of the saddle. The mare immediately stopped.

"Randy!" Gillian cried out, "I didn't kick her. She wasn't supposed to move."

Randy only laughed and told her to try again.

In a short while, Gillian felt quite comfortable about riding, and Randy said that they still had time to take a short trail ride before she would be needed back at the kitchen. He mounted another horse and started off across the corral where a trail led off into the trees.

Gillian was excited about the idea and followed right behind. It was not long before they were riding across a meadow covered with wild grasses and flowers.

"Would you like to walk for a while?" Randy called over his shoulder.

"Sure," Gillian answered and pulled Miss Polly to a stop.

It was a beautiful day. There was a slight breeze, but only enough to toss the grass gently and carry the scent of the flowers across the meadow.

Gillian climbed down and led Miss Polly to where Randy was standing.

"Where do I leave her?"

"We'll tie them over by that clump of trees."

After the horses had been securely tied, Randy told Gillian to follow him. He led her across the meadow to a spring that formed a gurgling little pool among the trees. They sat down beside the spring, enjoying the beautiful surroundings.

"It's so picturesque here," Gillian stated.

"That's a college word," Randy rebuffed, grinning.

"Sorry, I forgot you're just a wrangler," Gillian smiled.

"Never say 'just a wrangler,' " Randy said in a stern-sounding voice, and then laughed.

"Where does this spring go?" Gillian asked after a moment.

"I'm not sure. Maybe back underground and maybe into another stream."

"Let's follow it," Gillian suggested impulsively.

"We don't have any idea where it goes," Randy answered.

"There's only one way to find out," Gillian called over her shoulder and started off into the trees.

"Hey," Randy cried after her, "don't go without me! You'll get lost."

They followed the stream for some time and found that it eventually joined another stream. The new stream was quite large, but Gillian's curiosity was still not satisfied.

"Where do you suppose this one goes?" she asked casually.

"Oh no!" Randy warned, "we're not going any farther."

"Well, I'll see you back at camp then," Gillian said as she ran on.

"This is getting old," Randy muttered and started off after her again.

By the time he caught up, the stream had started down a steep hill. It cascaded and trickled over the rocks in its path like a thousand little elfs playing on the hill.

"Gillian," Randy said with finality in his voice, "I'm going back."

"Okay. But someday I'm coming back here to find out where that stream goes."

Randy looked at Gillian thoughtfully. The slight breeze tossed her hair gently as she stood gazing at the waterfall. He smiled to himself and answered, "Maybe we will."

Slowly they started back up the hill along the stream, realizing they had gone much farther than either had thought. By the time they reached the meadow, the sky was beginning to gray. Gillian realized it was far too late. She should have been in the kitchen by now. They quickly mounted their horses, and Randy set off at an uncomfortably fast pace for Gillian, who was not yet completely at ease on her horse. Her throat tightened as she thought of what she might find when she got back.

Just as they arrived at the stables, Jake appeared around the corner of the stalls and called out to them.

"Gillian, where have you been? We were worried about you. You were supposed to be in the kitchen an hour ago."

At this news, Gillian became frantic. She jumped down from her horse and tossed the reins to Randy, then started off at a brisk run down the path to the camp.

When she reached the kitchen, she took a deep breath and hurried inside. Kate was there, but the meal did not seem to be going well under her supervision. With a humble apology, Gillian took over, giving out directions and beginning some of the cooking herself to make up for her tardiness. There were only fifteen minutes until the doors were to be opened. In no way could the meal be ready by then.

Dinner began twenty minutes later than usual and, although few people complained openly, Gillian felt terrible. As soon as the clean-up was through, Kate asked to speak to her.

"Why were you late?" she began quietly.

"I'm very sorry, Kate. Randy was teaching me to ride, and we lost track of the time. It won't happen again, I promise."

"I don't think we've been fair to you," Kate continued, to Gillian's surprise. "We've expected you to be here every day, and a person just can't function that way without a break. Do you think there is someone else who could take over for you twice a week?"

Gillian couldn't believe her ears. "You mean I'd get two days off a week?"

"Most people do," Kate answered.

"Sharon could do it, I'm sure," Gillian said enthusiastically.

"Yes, I believe she could," Kate agreed. "Which days would you like?"

"It doesn't matter at all," Gillian answered.

"Then we'll give you Saturdays and Wednesdays."

"Thanks a lot, Kate," Gillian said sincerely. "I just don't know what to say. I am really sorry."

"You're forgiven. I know it won't happen again. I don't suppose we can talk Sharon into working tomorrow at such short notice, so you'll have to be here one last Saturday."

"I don't mind!" Gillian exclaimed quickly.

As she left the kitchen that night Gillian found herself humming. Life was wonderful. How could it get any better?

7

As the weeks rushed by, Gillian happily settled in to her new lifestyle. Each morning seemed to shine with the promise of new possibilities, and she found it easy to rise and explore them.

One evening, after a long day at work, as Gillian walked down the path she met Jake going the other direction.

"Where're you going, Gillian?"

"To my cabin," she answered cheerfully.

"I've missed you at vespers," Jake confided. "I was hoping you'd come back after that first time."

"It's not that I didn't like it," Gillian quickly responded. "I just haven't had the time," she finished lamely.

"Oh," Jake said quietly, "I see."

"I suppose I could come tonight."

"That would be great," Jake responded.

Gillian changed direction and walked back to the camp center with Jake. When they arrived, Sharon motioned to Gillian to come sit with her, and Jake took his place in the center of the circle of chairs.

Gillian enjoyed the singing and quickly picked up most of the tunes. When the last song was finished, Jake moved up behind the makeshift pulpit.

"Tonight I'm going to speak about a subject that is a little abstract," he began, "but if you'll just bear with me, I think you'll all get a great deal out of it.

"My scripture will be 1 Corinthians 2:6 through 9."

Gillian heard the shuffling sound of pages all around her, and Sharon quietly slid her Bible over so the two could share it.

"This is what the passage says. 'We do, however, speak a message of wisdom among the mature, but not the wisdom of this age or of the rulers of this age, who are coming to nothing. No, we speak of God's secret wisdom, a wisdom that has been hidden and that God destined for our glory before time began. None of the rulers of this age understood it, for if they had, they would not have crucified the Lord of glory. However, as it is written:

No eye has seen, nor ear has heard,
no mind has conceived what God has prepared
for those who love him.

"In many ways, we as humans feel now more than ever that we are wise. People have developed ways to do things that were never even dreamed about in the past. We have rockets that land on the moon, ships that dive into the deepest ocean depths, and television sets that let the whole world look on.

"It would be easy for us to say, 'I don't need God. I have myself and my knowledge.'

"In this passage we see that this has always been a problem with men and women. From the Tower of Babel to the crucifixion of Christ, human beings have felt self-sufficient. God has often had to remind us that we are only the creation and He is the Creator."

As Jake spoke, Gillian began to think back over her past. She had felt so proud of herself when they told her she was to be valedictorian. When her new job here at the camp had gone so well, and her education had been so useful, she had thought she knew it all. Now Jake was telling her that these things were really not important. How could he say that?

"I'm sure," Jake was saying, "that the leaders of the Jews had good intentions when they tried to rid their society of Jesus Christ. They must have tried very hard to believe He was simply another rebel trying to start another cult. And the people of the day certainly stood behind them.

"So they put Him to death, not an uncommon thing in those days. That's the worst thing they could have done to Him, right?

"Wrong. The people of Jesus' time at least dealt with the fact that Christ existed. Please don't take me wrong. I'm not saying that what they did was justified, but perhaps there is something worse. In modern times many have often ignored Him. They have tried their best to pretend they believe there is no God at all.

"I'm sure Christ would rather be dealt with than totally ignored."

Gillian began to squirm. Suddenly she had the feeling that God was very real. That He was looking straight at her and expecting to be reckoned with. The pressure built inside of her and she felt she somehow had to escape.

"Sharon," she whispered as calmly as she could, "I have to run back to the kitchen. I think I left a burner on."

Sharon looked up with questioning eyes, but smiled and moved so that Gillian could slip out. Gillian's heart raced as she walked past the questioning eyes around her and, once outside the door, fled across the yard to the kitchen.

There was no real reason to run to the kitchen, but she had always been taught not to lie, so her guilt drove her to act out her excuse for leaving the meeting.

When she entered, she stopped with a sigh of relief. It was safe here, as if once again she was accountable to no one but herself. The pressure she had felt earlier seemed to disappear.

"Isn't it a little late for you to be working?" a voice drawled from behind her.

Gillian's head snapped around in surprise, then relief as she saw it was only Randy.

"I'm just checking to see that the burners are off," she responded quickly—too quickly.

"I saw you take off from vespers," he stated frankly. "That's why I followed you here. You see, I went through that stage, too. Don't worry about it. It'll pass."

"What do you mean?" Gillian asked, blushing.

"Well, when I started working here two years ago, I felt like everybody was pushing me into their religious mold, too. It's not a pleasant feeling but it wears off. They eventually give up and just learn to live with you the way you are."

"You mean you're not—"Gillian stumbled—"religious?"

"No," Randy said candidly, "I don't need it. I have decided that some people aren't sure of themselves, so if they can believe that there is some sort of god that is watching over them, they feel more stable. Do you know what I mean?"

"I guess so. You're saying that religion is for people who are insecure?"

"Maybe not insecure," he replied slowly, "just not too sure of themselves."

A sudden thought provoked Gillian slightly. "Jake is not insecure, but he's religious."

"He just hides it well. Some of them can do that. But in the end, why else would an intelligent man turn to a myth?"

"Maybe it's not a myth," she shot back, upset that Randy thought Jake was less than perfect. She may not have believed in his God, but she certainly believed in Jake.

"Well," Randy said sarcastically, "I see they've got you just about hooked."

"I didn't say I believed it and I didn't say I didn't," she snapped hotly and turned quickly to leave the room.

"You know what the next step is?" Randy called after her. "You start lying awake nights and having bad dreams. You just wait. You'll start feeling the guilt trip any time now."

Gillian was a long way from the kitchen before her nerves calmed down enough to enable her to think. Randy had infuriated her with his condescending attitude.

She walked past her cabin and on down the path. She walked away from the camp, leaving Randy and Jake behind and, she struggled to convince herself, the God who seemed to be trying so hard to speak to her.

It was a long time before Gillian slowed down. She didn't seem to notice how dark the sky was getting or how cold the night was. Her mind was still racing and her feet seemed to be trying to keep up with it.

When she finally felt a cold chill, she was jerked back to reality. As she looked around, nothing seemed familiar. The path had long since disappeared, and the trees hid any view of the surrounding area. She was suddenly struck by a horrible thought. She was lost!

All at once fears swept into her mind. She remembered what Kyle had told her about the bears, and the other stories she had heard long ago about people freezing to death in the snow. The fact that there was no snow did not seem to comfort her at all. She simply imagined that it could fall suddenly from the sky and cover her.

She began to run, trying to escape the fears, but they followed her. Uncontrollably, she ran deeper and deeper into the forest, but she couldn't seem to hide from them. The fears now took on the form of some fierce and unknown beast chasing her, and the faster she ran the larger and more ferocious the beast became.

At last she could run no more and she threw herself down at the base of a tree to face whatever was following her. As she turned to look behind her, she was almost surprised to find nothing there.

Suddenly, in the midst of her anguish, she heard a quiet voice. It had no real substance. It was more of a feeling than something audible. The voice said, "Don't be afraid. I'm with you."

At any other time in her life, Gillian would have been more frightened by this voice than by any of the dangers she had imagined earlier, but now she was somehow comforted by it. The words seemed to push aside all her other thoughts, replacing them with a gentle peace.

She had not sat by the tree for long before she heard her name called. At first she didn't answer, imagining that it was still the voice she had heard before. Then suddenly she realized that this voice belonged to Kyle.

"I'm here," she called back.

"Gillian, what on earth are you doing out here?" Kyle asked when he reached her.

She lowered her head, feeling very foolish. "I got lost," she said pitifully.

Kyle leaned over and took her hand to help her up. As she looked up, she saw his eyes searching hers and her gaze dropped again.

"Why are you walking alone? Jake was worried sick when he saw you leave so fast. He couldn't leave the meeting so he sent me to look for you."

Gillian couldn't answer. She couldn't seem to remember what had made her so frightened in the first place and she was not certain that she had really heard the voice at all.

"Let's walk back to my cabin," Kyle said quietly, turning to lead the way.

The two had walked only a short distance when Gillian

saw Kyle's cabin. Realizing she had been only a hundred feet from safety made her feel extremely ridiculous. What would Kyle think of a girl who said she was lost just a few feet from his doorstep? She must have walked all the way around the small lake and stopped just before she would have recognized her surroundings.

When they were inside, Kyle offered Gillian a chair and busied himself making hot chocolate.

As he sat down and placed the two steaming mugs in front of them, he began softly, "Would you like to talk about it?"

"I'm not sure how it happened anymore," Gillian answered slowly. "One minute I was just walking and the next I thought I was lost. I guess I panicked."

"Are you sure that's all there is to it?" he prodded.

"Not really," Gillian whispered as all of the emotions surfaced and she began to cry.

Kyle let her cry for a few moments and then, placing his hand gently on hers, asked if she could tell him what was really bothering her.

Through sniffles and tears, Gillian repeated the whole episode to him. She started with vespers and then told him what Randy had said, how confused she was, and then about her fears and the voice that she now questioned.

Kyle listened intently and then waited for a moment before he responded.

"I believe, Gillian, that you are under conviction. Do you know what that means?"

At the shake of her head he went on. "That means that God is attempting to speak to you about things that are wrong in your life that keep you from knowing Him as your Father. He wants to have you as one of His children, and He's going to try very hard to move you toward that decision."

"But why me?" Gillian broke in. "Why not somebody

else? Randy doesn't feel like this and I'm sure there are others. Why pick on me?"

"He's not 'picking on you.' He's letting you know that He loves you very much and He doesn't want to lose you. Perhaps Randy is not ready, or he may have stopped listening altogether. God is dealing with many other people as well but not always in the same way. The important thing to realize is that God is trying to speak to you because He loves you. He loves you so much that He sent His only Son to die for you. I'm sure you've heard that before, but do you realize just what it means? God became man and lived and died just so that people like you and me could be made acceptable to enter heaven. And yet, for many people that just isn't enough. It's a lucky thing that He never gives up on us. He continues to do whatever He can to convince us of our need for Him."

"That's what He was doing? When I felt so afraid and He calmed me down, He was trying to say that I need Him?" Her thoughts went back to what Randy had said about religion being for people who were not sure of themselves. It seemed that if she accepted what Kyle was saying, she was admitting that she could not survive on her own.

"I'm just not sure, Kyle," she said after some time. "I need to think about this some more."

"That's fine, Gillian, but don't wait until it's too late. We never know what will happen tomorrow."

Kyle offered to walk her back to her cabin, but Gillian declined. She felt foolish enough to have caused him to go looking for her late at night. She just wanted to be alone.

As she crawled into bed that night, she whispered quietly, "If you're really there, God, please don't stop trying to talk to me. It's not that I don't want to believe in you; it's just very hard."

8

The days went by quickly and Gillian found herself busy keeping up with the endless number of campers pouring in. To make matters worse, Sharon became ill and Gillian was forced to run the kitchen every day for two weeks. When at last Sharon was back on her feet and able to work, Gillian was exhausted and ready for a rest.

Kate told her to take three days off, which she was more than willing to accept. As she walked back to her cabin after her last day of work, Gillian's mind wandered over the list of possibilities for the next three days, reveling in the knowledge that she could choose to do anything she wanted.

Since it was still early evening, Gillian changed her clothes, then walked out to sit and think on the low-hanging tree limb she had found on her first day by the lake. She had often come back to that spot in the evenings and found it a peaceful place to sit and reflect on the day's events. As she sat contentedly, she heard a voice call her name and she quickly answered. Jake appeared out of the bushes and walked up beside her, smiling.

"I thought I'd find you out here. From now on, it's the first place I'll look."

"Isn't it a beautiful night, Jake?" she said dreamily.

"One of the nicest," he answered wholeheartedly. "Say, everyone's getting together tomorrow afternoon for some water sports. We'd all be very pleased if you'd join us."

The staff often used Sunday afternoon as a time to free

themselves from the pressures of the week. Gillian had been too busy the last few weeks to join them and now was very excited at the chance to be a part of the fun.

"Where are you going to meet and when should I show up?" she asked, not bothering to mask her enthusiasm.

"We meet at the river crossing at one o'clock. And dress in something you don't mind getting wet."

"I'll be there!" Gillian replied with a grin, and Jake went off to inform the others.

The next afternoon, Gillian met Kate on the way to the river and they discussed the plans for the next week. By the time they arrived, many of the staff were already there, and the crowd buzzed with excitement.

Since it seemed that most of those who were expected had arrived, John Phillips, Kate's husband, jumped onto a stump and explained the rules. Gillian had never heard of the game before.

It was fashioned after football but had some very unusual twists. For one, it was played with a watermelon covered with a thick layer of grease. The group was divided into two teams, with the river as the playing field. The object of the game was for one team to get the greased melon to their side of the river while the other team fought to steal it and take it to the other side. It seemed easy to Gillian at first, but she soon realized that holding on to a wet, greased watermelon was anything but simple.

The ice-cold mountain water was only waist-deep, but everyone was soon thoroughly wet and chilled to the bone. Each of them jumped out often to warm up.

As the melon went back and forth, never quite reaching either shore, laughter filled the air. When someone had the "ball," everyone else dunked him in an effort to steal it. Gillian and some of the other women stood back for the most part and watched the group of men and a few energetic women push and shove each other in an effort to get at the melon.

Suddenly the melon was jarred from someone's arms and thrown high into the air, landing with a splash in front of Gillian. For a moment she stood, uncertain what to do, and then hearing the cheers from those around her, she picked up the melon and made a dash for her shore.

Too late, she saw Kyle flying toward her. With one final attempt she lunged toward the shore just as Kyle pushed her under the water. She felt the melon slip from her hands and shoot away. When she jumped up, she saw that it had landed just out of reach for both Kyle and herself. The two made a quick leap and the watermelon sank to the bottom, splitting on rocks beneath them.

When they stood up, Kyle had a chunk of melon in each hand and stains down his T-shirt. Gillian felt guilty for ruining the game, but no one around seemed upset. Then Kyle started to laugh and shout something about her hair.

Her hand shot up to find what was wrong and she felt chunks of melon and seeds all through it. When she realized she must look even worse than Kyle, she began to laugh harder and the whole group joined in.

In no time John brought out another melon and the game began again. Gillian washed the melon out of her hair as best she could in the icy river and then sat on the bank in the warm sunshine to watch.

When the other melon was destroyed too, the game was over and Gillian's team was declared the losers. The players got out of the water after splashing and teasing some more and dried themselves off. As the group walked back to their cabins, Kyle caught up to Gillian.

"You aren't one to hold a grudge, are you?" he asked playfully.

"Not me," Gillian answered, laughing. "But wait until next time."

"Hey," he continued after chuckling, "I hear that you've got a free day tomorrow. Would you be interested in riding with Randy and me and some campers in the morning?"

"I sure would!" she exclaimed. "Where are you going?"

"We'll be taking a couple of men to the cable crossing where they're going to be picked up by a private plane. The ride is terribly long, but the scenery is wonderful. I know you'll enjoy it."

"Oh, I will! I'll be at the stables bright and early."

"I'll be looking for you," Kyle answered and walked away in the direction of his cabin.

Gillian spent the rest of the afternoon writing letters home. In the last couple of weeks she had not had the time to write, and she was sure her parents and friends were feeling neglected.

When it was time for dinner, Gillian bounced off her bed and quickly changed her clothes. She was looking forward to seeing what Sharon would fix for the meal, since she was planning the menu as well as supervising its preparation.

As Gillian walked down the path, she met Jake, who was also on his way to the dining room.

"Good evening, miss. How would you like an escort?" Jake asked Gillian cordially.

"I'd like that very much, kind sir," Gillian responded with a lopsided curtsy, and they both laughed.

Sharon had planned a delicious meal and Gillian was impressed. It was such a good feeling to be able to take her days off without worrying about the kitchen.

Jake was in very good spirits during dinner, making the time very enjoyable for Gillian.

"How did you like the game today?" he asked.

"I liked it a lot. Whoever came up with such a crazy idea?"

"I'm not really sure whose idea it was, but it caught on a few years back and we've kept it around ever since."

After the meal, Jake walked Gillian back to her cabin and they stood for a moment looking across the lake. The orange glow of the setting sun shimmered across the water, leaving a trail of shadowy light.

"Do you know when it's easiest for me to believe in God, Jake?" Gillian asked thoughtfully.

"When?"

"When I look around me and see all the incredible things in the world. I studied evolution in school and really tried to believe it, but somehow I was never satisfied. The world is too beautiful a place to believe that it's just a freak accident."

"I'm glad it isn't an accident," Jake agreed quietly. "I think I'd feel less important somehow. With God, I know that He put me here because He loves me very much.

"I've heard people say that Christians are insecure, but I think we are the most fulfilled group of people around. Knowing how much God loves me has helped me to be strong during many rough times in my life. Even if there was no reward after death, I wouldn't give up my relationship with God for a moment."

Gillian was relieved that Jake had just refuted Randy's theory. Then her thoughts toyed with a new idea. "But isn't it really hard trying to be a good person and do what's right all the time? Don't you ever feel like it's hopeless?" asked Gillian.

"Sometimes I do," Jake answered honestly. "But then I realize I can't do it on my own. That's what is so wonderful about having a daily, close relationship with Jesus Christ. Only He has the power to help me make the right choices. He gives me strength to live the way I should. That's the part I wouldn't give up. I know that people who don't have Christ often have a problem with feeling alone and unloved, but I never have to feel that way. God never lets me down."

That night as Gillian got ready for bed, she thought about Jake's words. He made religion seem so different from what she had always pictured it. To Jake, being a Christian was not a list of do's and don'ts. It was something that made his life better. At times Gillian knew she could use a reassuring feeling like that. Maybe someday she would try Jake's way and see how she liked it. For now, she didn't feel as if she was ready to commit herself.

9

As Gillian dressed the next morning, she hummed softly to herself. Kyle had asked her to spend the day with him. Carefully she pulled her special blue sweater out of the drawer. When her mother had insisted they buy it, Gillian had thought she would never wear it at the camp. Now Gillian wanted Kyle to notice her. Perhaps the beautiful sweater would help.

Randy called out to Gillian as soon as she turned the corner at the stables, and she cheerfully returned his greeting. She helped him feed the horses and then asked where she could find Kyle.

"He's out in the corral with one of the mares," Randy answered. "She's lame and he thinks he knows why."

Gillian ran across the yard and was about to call Kyle's name when she saw him stooping over the raised hoof of the mare she had ridden for her first lesson. Seeing that he was busy, she crawled up onto the fence and sat watching him, unseen.

She noticed how gentle he was with the horse and how softly he spoke to help keep her calm. Her mind went back to the watermelon game, and she realized how different he was now. Not only could this man be competitive and outgoing, but gentle and caring as well. Her mind drifted back to the night he had found her in the woods. She remembered how easily she had poured out her feelings to him. She knew few people like that. In fact, Krystal and her mother were the only ones whom Gillian considered close enough to confide in.

Somehow this tall, handsome stranger had slipped quietly into her confidence. At that moment, she understood what a wonderful friend she had found and she was grateful.

At last Kyle looked up and noticed Gillian watching him.

"Hi there," he called to her. "How are you feeling this morning?"

"Wonderful," she answered and then added, "what's wrong with Miss Polly?"

"Nothing that a good rest won't cure," he responded, setting down the hoof and walking over to Gillian. "She had a stone jammed under her shoe and the cut became infected. I had to take the shoe off and clean it out, but she'll be fine in no time at all."

Gillian looked over at the mare and sighed in relief.

"Are you ready to set off into the great outdoors?" Kyle asked, smiling.

"I thought that's where I have been for weeks," Gillian laughed back.

"Not like you will be today," he said convincingly. "We're going to ride down that cutline and head north for a few miles." As he spoke he pointed toward a road-like space cleared of trees leading up the side of a mountain just across the valley from them.

"I wondered what that was. What's it for?"

"It's used by most people for easier travel and also a directional guide because it always runs true to the points of the compass, but it was made as a protection against rampant forest fires. That's a major problem because if the season is dry and a fire starts it's difficult to get the equipment needed all the way back here to put it out. They spread so quickly in a forest like this."

"It's a good idea, then."

"Obviously someone thought so," remarked Kyle with a chuckle and walked over to the stables. Gillian followed close behind.

The campers soon arrived and they set out on the ride. Gillian lost herself in the glory of her surroundings, and they rode on in silence.

It was a cool day, but the warm sun, the gentle breeze, and the pure joy of being outdoors made Gillian feel happy to be alive. The sky was almost cloudless above the mountains rising clear and solid all around her. The ride took them into a deep valley and high onto the side of a neighboring mountain, then deep into the trees. Gillian enjoyed it all, but her favorite part was when they rode beside a steep, rocky hill where a small waterfall played over the rocks. She remembered the falls she and Randy had found. A sparkling waterfall had always been fascinating to her.

By the time they arrived at the river crossing, Gillian was completely lost in her thoughts and did not notice that they were stopping until her horse, on its own initiative, stopped abruptly.

"You going to keep going right into the river?" Randy called teasingly.

Gillian dismounted quickly and tried to hide her embarrassment. No one seemed to notice, so she tied her horse to a tree and followed the men.

Just as they walked over the top of a slight incline, Gillian saw something she had never seen before. Large cables stretched from the edge of a cliff on one side of the river to a tower on the other. Hanging from the cables was a cart of some kind. Its wooden frame was just large enough for two seats, holding four people. The small cart hung on two pulley wheels running along the cable. Ropes, tied to either side of the cart and extending to the tower and cliff, were used to pull it from side to side.

It was a dangerous-looking contraption, and Gillian

held her breath as the two men they had escorted got into the car. Then Kyle and Randy pushed the cart out over the river where it swung precariously. Slowly the men were drawn to the other side, where they disembarked. They climbed down from the tower and, after waving goodbye to their escorts, walked off toward a cabin set back into the trees to wait for their ride home.

"What's the matter, Gillian?" Randy grinned. "Haven't you ever seen a cable cart before?" His tone implied that everyone had.

"Randy," Kyle answered for her, "there isn't much need of one in the city, now is there?"

"Guess not," Randy answered, looking at Kyle with a slight frown.

"What if you fall out when you're in the middle?" Gillian asked with a white face. Her thoughts were not on Randy but on the cables swaying far above the churning water.

"You don't fall out," Kyle answered patiently, "because the seats are set down into the cart. Why don't we pull it back so you can take a better look?"

Randy and Kyle pulled the cart back across the river. Without the weight of people in it, the wind tossed the cart, making Gillian feel even more uncertain.

When the cart was safely grounded on the cliff, Gillian stepped cautiously up to it and looked inside. Kyle was right. The seats sunk into the cart, but only by about ten inches.

"Want to give it a shot?" Randy said, laughing, trying once more to pull Gillian's attention to himself. "I bet you wouldn't even sit in it when it's grounded, let alone when it's clear out over the water."

The jeering tone in Randy's voice made Gillian's temper rise. Without thinking first, she climbed into the cart and sat glaring up at Randy triumphantly.

Randy was startled at Gillian's sudden anger, but since he was uncertain how to amend the problem, he continued, "Well, what do you know? The lady isn't so green after all."

"That's enough, Randy," Kyle interrupted before things got out of hand. Then he changed the subject quickly. "Would you like to ride it out a little way?"

"Only if you come out with me, Kyle," Gillian said innocently.

Randy's mouth fell open and he knew for the moment that he had lost.

Kyle climbed into the cart beside Gillian, and Randy pushed them out over the river. Just as the cart left the platform, Gillian let out a muffled cry and Randy saw Kyle take her hand. Anger burned inside him. Earlier that day he had told Kyle how he was beginning to feel about Gillian and Kyle had not seemed to want to listen. Now he realized the reason for Kyle's seeming indifference. Kyle also had feelings for Gillian. It seemed to Randy that he would lose out and the thought made him all the more upset.

When Kyle and Gillian had reached midstream, a wicked thought flashed into Randy's mind. Casually he dropped the rope he had been pulling and the cart glided to a stop. Stepping up and grabbing the cable from which the cart hung, he began to push and pull at it, causing the cart to swing.

Gillian and Kyle tried desperately to call to him, but he pretended not to hear them and continued to swing the cable. The cart tossed higher and higher and Gillian froze in her seat. Kyle knew the cart would not fall, but he was afraid for Gillian's sake. Her expression showed how frightened she really was.

Finally, Randy lost interest and stopped swinging on the cable. Suddenly feeling very immature, he tossed an angry look in Kyle's direction and walked away from the scene, not daring to look back.

Kyle struggled to pull the cart manually along the cables. It took a great deal of effort, but at last they were safely back on the cliff. Kyle helped Gillian from the cart to a seat on the soft moss under a tree.

"Stay here, Gillian," Kyle said with a deep breath, "I'll be right back." Then he went off in search of Randy.

Kyle found him by the horses, lying under a tree. Randy looked up at him as if nothing had happened, then turned his back to Kyle.

"That was stupid, Randy!" Kyle said, forcing himself to keep his anger down.

"I knew you wouldn't get hurt," was his only answer.

"I knew we wouldn't too, but Gillian didn't. She was terrified out there." Then he paused. "Why did you do it?"

Randy jerked himself to his feet and looked Kyle squarely in the face. "How can you say that?" he shouted. "I told you how I feel about Gillian and now you steal her from under my nose. You've got a lot of nerve asking me that!"

"I didn't steal her, Randy," Kyle began slowly and painfully. "The way things stand, Gillian and I can't be anything more than mere friends."

"How's that?" Randy asked, taken aback.

"Gillian is not a Christian," Kyle answered reluctantly. He had been telling himself for some time that she would soon make a decision for God, but it had not happened. Now he was trying to force himself to accept the fact that she may never make that choice. It was difficult for him. He continued awkwardly, "Although I think she is a wonderful person, I cannot allow myself to become seriously involved with an unbeliever. The Bible warns against such relationships."

Randy laughed back. "So you think you're better than her. Well, it doesn't look like she feels the same about you."

"No, I don't think I'm better than she is. It's not always

easy for me to live by that standard, but I know I want to try."

"Then you're leaving her to me, right?" Randy wanted a definite answer. "You won't try to get in the way?"

"Unless the situation changes, I will continue to be her friend but nothing more," Kyle said with pain in his voice. He turned quickly to walk away, but Randy's expression was still skeptical.

The ride back to camp was slow and quiet. No one seemed to be able to talk. Gillian was still trembling from her ride, and the two men were deep in their own thoughts.

When they finally arrived, Gillian left hurriedly, while Kyle and Randy silently labored over the evening chores.

As Gillian climbed into bed that night, she whispered quietly, "Thank you, God, for keeping us safe today." She was not sure whether He would hear her short prayer, but she felt very grateful, indeed, and wanted with all her heart to try to express it.

10

The next morning Gillian dressed speedily, planning her day as she did. It was the last day of her short holiday and she wanted to use it effectively.

It did not take her long to realize she had little with which to fill her day. She had caught up on all her correspondence on Sunday, and she was far ahead of herself in her personal chores. This left little for her to do with the day ahead of her. At last she decided to walk into camp and from there decide what to do with her time.

She was ambling slowly along the path still looking for an activity when she saw Jake walking up behind her with a fishing rod in his hand.

"Jake," she called out, "are you going fishing?"

"No," he answered, "a friend asked to borrow my rod and I'm taking it down to him."

"That's too bad," answered Gillian disheartedly.

"What's the matter?"

"I just can't find anything to do today."

"Well, that's easily remedied. Why don't you come with me? I'm driving down to the Okanagan Valley, and that will take most of the day. Would you like to come along?"

"That would be wonderful!" exclaimed Gillian. "When are you leaving?"

"Just as soon as I deliver this fishing rod."

"I'll come with you then. I'm ready to go anywhere."

The two had had little opportunity lately for a long talk

and they both found they missed it. Jake explained to Gillian that he was going to pick up some fruit which could not be shipped by mail from the prosperous valley.

In no time at all they were driving through the gate, heading toward the Okanagan. Gillian knew the trip would be long, so she relaxed against the worn car seat. It was Jake's car and he treasured it, even when most other people would have traded it in. He said it had many good memories tied to it.

When Gillian told him about the day before, he chuckled to himself. He could easily see why Randy had acted the way he had, even though it was a mystery to Gillian. He quickly shifted the conversation to other things.

"How is it that you came to the camp?" Jake began.

"My father knows Kate's father, and when I couldn't find a job back home, Dad started doing some looking for me. Mr. Jeffery told him about the camp and it seemed as if it was my only choice." Gillian chuckled as she realized for the first time how different her new world was from what she had expected.

"I was so scared to come here," Gillian said softly.

"Why is that?"

"I pictured a desolate place with nothing but rough men and snow all year. I was sure I wouldn't ever have a friend—especially not a close one. And I was just as sure I'd never learn to feel comfortable in the mountains."

"And how do you feel now?"

Gillian looked out the window for a moment, trying to see deep enough inside of herself to be able to answer Jake. "I do feel comfortable now. In fact, I really like it here. And I have a few good friends. That was probably the hardest part, though. I'm not used to having to make friends and I still feel awkward sometimes."

"You seem to be fitting in well, Gillian," Jake noted. "When do you feel uncomfortable?"

"Not with you," laughed Gillian. "Sometimes it feels as if I've always known you." She paused for a moment before continuing. "I guess it's mostly with the people at work. I never know how to treat Kate. She's so easygoing that I'm sure we could be friends. There is just something that makes me feel restrained around her. After all, she is my boss, and I should show some respect for her.

"And when I'm the one in charge in the kitchen, I feel awkward, too. I've never been one to tell people what to do. Half the time I feel like I'm being bossy and demanding, and the other half I'm scared to even make a suggestion for fear of being misunderstood. Nobody else seems to notice, but I'm just so self-conscious around them. I don't know how to make myself relax."

Jake smiled as if remembering something from his past and then answered Gillian. "It's always difficult to strike a balance between respect and over-familiarity with authority. Whether it's you looking up to Kate or the kitchen workers and their view of you, often only time can make attitudes fit into their proper place. Don't be discouraged if you feel strange for a while. Pretty soon you'll know what to expect from those around you, and they'll know what to expect from you. Just have patience and keep trying. I'm sure you're sensitive enough to make things work."

"But how long will it take?" asked Gillian earnestly.

"I won't lie to you. Sometimes it takes a long time. Probably each of the relationships will take a different amount of time. Just keep thinking about the ones that are already working themselves out. If you become too anxious about waiting, it often makes everything more difficult in the long run."

Suddenly Gillian felt a need for a confidant. "Jake," she whispered, "maybe I don't have that long to let things go. To be honest, I'm only planning to stay here for a year and then find another job. It's not that I don't like it here," she hurried to stress the point. "I just want to get back home to my family and friends."

"Oh," Jake acknowledged. Silence hung over the car for a moment before he continued, "I would be sorry to see you leave, Gillian. And I know there are others who would feel the same way. You're really sincere about your job. I know John and Kate appreciate that. And everyone at the watermelon game enjoyed your good-natured spirit and enthusiasm. A lot of us here consider you our friend."

"Thanks, Jake," Gillian answered softly. "I needed to hear that." Gillian sat gazing thoughtfully out the window. There really weren't too many problems. Maybe she should consider staying indefinitely A year was not very long, and she was sure there would be many pleasant days to fill her time. But how would she tell her family? Could she really leave them for longer than a year?

At last they drove onto a side road and, after several miles, pulled into a winding lane that stopped in front of an old house. The house was small and looked as if it might fall over, but it had a friendly atmosphere which Gillian liked. The cluttered yard was scattered with farm implements, and three large dogs ran back and forth across it.

Before they were even out of the car, an elderly woman hurried from the porch toward them. She had deep smile lines in a her face, and her gray hair was pulled up in a tight knot. A simple dress covered her stout frame, but her sparkling eyes made her seem beautiful.

"Jacob!" she cried, "it's been so long. Let me have a look at you."

"How have you been, Aunt Lucy? You look like a queen," Jake returned with equal enthusiasm. He hugged his aunt tightly and then kissed her softly on the cheek.

"Oh, you flatter me so. But who is this young lady you've brought with you?" and without waiting for an answer, she reached out and hugged Gillian, too.

"This is Gillian Todd, Aunt Lucy," Jake answered. "She's one of the staff at our camp. She came along with me to see how good fruit is grown."

"Welcome, dear," Aunt Lucy said. "God bless you."

Gillian was somewhat uncertain for a moment, but before she could feel awkward, Aunt Lucy had ushered her into the house.

The inside of the house was not much tidier than the yard, but it looked very comfortable. Gillian noticed the pictures covering an entire wall in the living room and spreading across the top of the piano. *Wow*, she thought, *she sure has a love for people.*

"I've been so anxious to see you, Jacob," Aunt Lucy was saying. "When I heard the dogs barking, I knew it would be you this time and I couldn't restrain myself."

"What do you mean 'this time'?" Jake asked inquisitively.

"Well," Aunt Lucy paused with a blush, "young Pastor Simmons came out unexpectedly. I heard his car coming and I ran out all in a dither because I thought it was you. I don't suppose he has ever been greeted so enthusiastically by one of his church members. I made quite a fool of myself, shouting and waving. You see, in my excitement, I didn't stop for my glasses, and I'd hugged him three times before I realized it wasn't you. Then we were both so embarrassed that he said he'd come back some other time."

Jake's hearty laughter filled the room, and although Gillian tried to politely keep herself from laughing, she could not stifle a giggle.

Aunt Lucy didn't seem to mind. She laughed right along with them and then hustled off to put on the coffee pot. Amid cookies, coffee, and Aunt Lucy's delightful chatter, Gillian began to feel perfectly at ease.

Aunt Lucy had an immense orchard and garden. She grew all types of fruit and vegetables, then sold them to local businesses. In fact, this farm was the major supplier for the camp itself. Her late husband, who was Jake's father's brother, had set up the farm many years before, and after he died Aunt Lucy had kept it up. Many well-intentioned neighbors had advised her to sell the farm, but she adamantly refused. She simply hired more workers and made plans for a new peach orchard.

Gillian could tell that Aunt Lucy was not the kind of person to let life's stress break her. The farm had been productive and Aunt Lucy lived a full life here, where she felt she belonged.

After their lunch, Aunt Lucy showed them the grounds. Trees stretched farther than the eye could see, and the garden was so large that there seemed to be no end to it. People hurried to and fro, tending to their jobs. Gillian noticed how cheerfully Aunt Lucy greeted each person by name, bringing a smile to many faces.

"Marvin," Aunt Lucy called to one of the young men, "load the boxed produce from the shed into Jake's car."

"Yes, ma'am," Marvin answered respectfully and set off to do as he was told.

"I'll go help him," Jake put in quickly. "You ladies go on up to the house and I'll meet you there soon."

Aunt Lucy continued to chatter all the way to the house, and Gillian was more than content to listen to the interesting woman. By the time the men arrived, Aunt Lucy had covered several subjects thoroughly and was beginning another.

"Isn't it wonderful the way the good Lord blesses those of us who love Him? Don't you feel His love around you all of the time, child?"

Caught off guard, Gillian, at a loss for words, struggled for something to say in return.

"You mean you don't know His blessing in your life?" Aunt Lucy asked without a hint of accusation. Gillian felt that she could be completely candid.

"I don't really understand about God. I've been learning some, but I have so many questions."

"There are always questions, Gillian," Aunt Lucy said with a knowing nod, "but that's the wonder of our Father. He tells us we don't need to understand everything. All we need is faith to accept it. We're human and we can't expect to know as God does. But we can know that He will always do what's best for us and that He will never leave us to ourselves. It's wonderful to know that. I wouldn't trade it for all of the other knowledge in the world."

"I've never heard it explained that way before. Isn't faith something religious people have worked for all their lives? How could I ever hope to be that good when people so much better than I am don't seem to make it?"

"Faith isn't something you earn," Aunt Lucy answered patiently. "It's something God allows you to have. Like a gift. He doesn't expect you to create it on your own. That's why you're fighting Him right now. You think that before you can accept Him, you have to feel you understand. Feelings don't really have anything to do with faith."

Gillian thought for a moment. Aunt Lucy made God seem like a trusted friend rather than the judge of all her sins. Gillian decided she liked that idea, though maybe it was just that Aunt Lucy could see the good side of everything. On the other hand, Gillian also believed Aunt Lucy was a very credible person. If she said something was true, then it must be. It was that simple.

The sound of the door closing brought Gillian back from her reflections. Jake entered the kitchen and said they were ready to set out.

"Do you have to leave so soon?" Aunt Lucy asked.

"I'm afraid we do."

"Well, if you must go, I'll let you," Aunt Lucy said resignedly, "but promise you'll try to stop by here again soon."

Jake promptly promised and Aunt Lucy turned expectantly to Gillian.

Seeing that she was expected to promise, too, Gillian quickly assured Aunt Lucy, making her smile warmly.

"And you don't need to wait for my nephew to bring you," she added with a twinkle in her eye. "Jacob thinks a person needs a reason to visit another. Don't you think that's silly?"

Gillian laughed and they all stepped out into the afternoon sun. They called goodbye one last time as they set off down the lane. Gillian decided then that she would return soon to visit Aunt Lucy.

"Your aunt is a wonderful lady," Gillian said thoughtfully.

"She certainly is," Jake agreed heartily. "She's been like a mother to me ever since mine passed away."

"When was that, Jake?"

"Oh, many years ago. Now, she was a woman I wish you could have met. She was tall and mean-looking if you stepped out of line, but as gentle as they come. My father married her when she was only sixteen years old, and she followed him all over this country.

"They grew up in Nova Scotia, both of them in the same county. They would have gone to school together, too, if my father hadn't been nine years older. By the time my mother was old enough to be finished with the seven-grade schoolhouse, my father had been to sea twice."

"Why did they move to Saskatchewan?" Gillian asked, wanting him to continue the story.

"They didn't move there at first. You see, on my father's last voyage he talked his younger brother into sailing with him, and my uncle was killed in a terrible storm. Papa was the one who had to tell his mother about the accident.

After that he couldn't bring himself to sail anymore.

"When his mother died two years later, he took Mama and moved to the city. They lived in Montreal for a number of years. That's where my older sister and I were born. But Mama became very ill and the doctor advised my father to take her to the country. He decided to try farming then, and they moved to Saskatchewan. That's where they settled and where I grew up."

"Were you ever married, Jake?"

"Yes," he answered slowly as if the memory might still be painful.

"You don't have to tell me about it if you don't want to," Gillian asserted quickly.

"I don't mind. It's just been so long since I've mentioned her. Most people know or just don't ask. Her name was Sarah. She was the prettiest little thing anyone could ever imagine. I couldn't believe my ears when she told me she'd go to the church social with me the first time I asked. All the boys fought over her." Jake paused for a moment, a far-off expression in his eyes.

"I fell in love with her that night. I think she liked me too, but she didn't show it. She made me woo her until I was blue in the face. Always pretending not to understand that I wanted to marry her.

"Then one night I got sick. I was so sick that the doctor and Sarah stayed by my bed night and day for a week. I don't remember much about that time except her cool hand on my forehead and her gentle voice coaxing me to get well.

"When I could sit up, she told me that she loved me and I proposed right then and there. We got married in the fall of the same year and lived happily together for thirty-eight years."

"Did you have any children?"

Jake smiled, his eyes glowing. "Did we have children? We had eight wonderful children. Of course, they're all leading lives of their own now. They scattered themselves all over this globe, so that I hardly get a chance to see them. Except Bess—she lives in Calgary and I see her quite often.

"My children have all matured into beautiful people. I'm a lucky man to have such a fine family."

"Yes, you are," Gillian agreed. "I'm an only child and always wished I had some brothers and sisters. I suppose I'd be a different person if I had."

"A large family certainly has its advantages, but it has its disadvantages, too. When hard times came, there were quite a few hungry mouths to feed. God helped us live through it, though, and we all learned to trust in Him for our daily bread."

There was silence in the car for a while and then Jake said, "We need to stop for gas. Would you like to find some place to eat supper too?"

"Sure," Gillian answered. "I'm getting pretty hungry."

The first familiar restaurant they saw was McDonald's and Jake pulled up to the drive-through window. The remaining miles were spent pleasantly eating Big Macs and sipping milk shakes while they shared more of their favorite memories.

Gillian sighed deeply as she lay in bed that night. She was so glad Jake had asked her to accompany him on the trip. He had made her last day off the best of all with his stories—a day Gillian knew she would remember for many years to come.

11

$\mathcal{I}$t was difficult for Gillian to begin work the next morning. Her mind kept wandering back to the things that had happened over the last three days, and it was hard for her to concentrate.

Kate stopped by early in the morning to chat awhile, and Gillian was more than willing to relate all the highlights of her time off, determined to try harder to befriend Kate.

By the time the noon meal was over, Gillian was ready to get out of the kitchen and find a place to relax. She ran to her cabin, changed clothes, and then went to sit by the lake and dangle her feet in the water.

As she was sitting there, her mind returned to Aunt Lucy and the way she had described faith. Could it be that simple?

Just as Gillian began reasoning out the concept, footsteps from behind caught her attention.

"What are you doing out here by yourself?" It was Randy.

"You startled me," Gillian answered. "I was just thinking."

"About who?" Randy asked slyly.

"Not about who—about what. I was just thinking about something I heard yesterday."

"Want to go for a walk?"

"I think I'd rather just sit for a while."

"Oh, come on. It'll be fun."

Gillian gave in and the two walked down a path that ran close to the lake. Randy talked continuously, but Gillian didn't mind. She wasn't listening, anyway. Her mind was on her inner struggles, and though Randy tried to pull her away from her thoughts, he had no success.

"You aren't paying attention, Gillian," Randy blurted out finally. His efforts to impress her with his knowledge had not been working well. He stopped short beside a little stream and said in desperation, "That's the third time I've asked you what kind of farming they do where you're from, and each time all you've done is nod your head. What's the matter with you?"

"Sorry. I'm just thinking," Gillian answered.

Randy decided to try again. As they sat down, he began to explain how a good dairy farm is set up. He was convinced that nobody could run one as well as his father. Gillian nodded occasionally but heard very little.

"A lot of people don't understand that," Randy continued. "It's very important to make sure that the cows don't eat too many weeds in the summer. Like I said, it spoils the quality of their milk."

"Uh-huh," Gillian answered.

"That's why milk usually tastes better in the winter. Farmers have to feed grain or hay to the cows, and they don't get anything that will make the milk taste bad."

"Uh-huh."

"Of course, store-bought milk is not the same. They do so much processing and treating to it that it's not even fit to drink when they're done."

"Uh-huh."

"Naturally, green milk tastes the best—especially if it has lumps in it."

"Uh-huh," Gillian answered, still distracted by her thoughts.

"Gillian!" cried Randy, finally losing his patience completely, "you haven't been listening to a word I've been saying!"

"I'm really sorry, Randy," she answered sincerely, climbing to her feet. "I'm just not having a very good day."

Randy quieted quickly and a determined look flashed over his face. "Maybe I could make your day a little better," he said, rising to stand in front of her and kissing her squarely.

Gillian jumped back and let out a disgusted cry. "Who do you think you are?" she cried as she pushed him away. Before he had time to catch himself, he stumbled backward over a rock and fell seat first into the middle of the little stream. Gillian threw him an angry look and strutted off down the path without looking back.

She walked directly back to her cabin. She did not even stop when Kyle called to her from across the clearing. She walked in, slammed the door, and threw herself into one of the chairs.

The nerve of that man! She could still see the grin on his face when he said he could make her day better. Maybe she had treated him poorly, but he had no right to do what he did. She had a mind to go right back to tell him exactly what she thought of him.

Suddenly she saw him in her mind's eye, sitting in the stream with his face scrunched up in surprise. The mental picture made her burst out in laughter.

There was a gentle knock on the door and she rose, still laughing, to answer it.

Kyle stood before her with a very surprised and confused look on his face. He had expected to find her crying or beating the walls with her fists by the way he had seen her walk across the grass. This fit of laughter made him uncertain how to respond.

"I was worried about you," he began slowly, eyeing Gillian carefully.

"I can take care of myself," Gillian answered and burst into laughter again as if she had just told a joke.

"You're sure there's nothing wrong?"

"I'm fine," she assured him, struggling for control.

"Okay," Kyle answered and turned slowly, glancing over his shoulder as he walked away.

Gillian closed the door and leaned against it. Kyle probably thought she was going crazy, but she couldn't stop laughing. Randy really had looked funny.

She calmed down and strolled down the path back to the kitchen, whistling. Suddenly she chuckled softly to herself. Randy had brightened her day after all.

12

Gillian decided to attend vespers that night and Jake was delighted. The message given was on the gifts of the Spirit, which Gillian found interesting. As she walked back to her cabin, she tried to guess what gifts each of her friends had. Jake said that everyone had been given at least one gift, but she was hard put to think of what some of their gifts would be. Jake, on the other hand, seemed to have them all.

As she walked she looked at the night around her. The moon was full, lighting the surrounding area with unusual brightness. The cool night air, though chilling, somehow made her feel intensely alive. The almost inaudible sound of little animals rustling in the bushes had become very familiar and almost a comfort. It meant that the world was vibrant and as full of life as she felt. The air held the delicious scent of an oncoming rain, and Gillian hoped there would be lightning and thunder as well. She loved to lie awake at night and hear the rain on the roof of her cabin. Let the lightning flash and the thunder boom; she would feel safe under the heavy quilt.

Before crawling into bed that night she picked up the Bible Jake had given her a few days before. She flipped through the pages and read the names of the books, struggling with some of them. They seemed very strange to her.

Finally she let it drop open and began to read different verses at random. One verse in particular held her attention.

It read, "When calamity comes, the wicked are brought down, but even in death the righteous have a refuge."

Gillian wondered at these words. They seemed to hold some hidden meaning she couldn't quite grasp. How could anyone have a refuge in the face of death? She had always believed that death was the final act in life; that no one could ever overcome it. How could this book of truth say it was something a person did not have to fear?

She laid the book on the table by her bed and resolved to ask Jake in the morning. The storm raged outside her tiny cabin, but Gillian slept soundly, unafraid of its fury.

The next morning she woke late and ran to make up for the time she had lost. She arrived in the kitchen just in time to give the orders for the preparation of breakfast and begin work herself.

Randy did not show up for breakfast. When Gillian asked Kyle about it, she was informed that he had complained of feeling ill since yesterday afternoon. Kyle supposed it was some sort of flu.

"More like injured pride," Gillian mumbled under her breath.

"What's that?" Kyle asked.

"Nothing."

Kyle eyed her carefully. She had been acting funny lately.

"By the way, Gillian," he said while helping himself to the pancakes, "I'm planning a short canoe trip downriver this Wednesday and I wondered if, since it's your day off, you might like to join me?"

Gillian accepted the offer quickly and Kyle said he would be looking forward to it.

That night as Gillian wrote a long letter to Krystal, telling her all about the last few days, she added an impulsive postscript.

"I have a feeling that this canoe trip is going to be very

important. Maybe this will be the time Kyle breaks the ice—at last. I hope so. Love, Gillian."

The next day went by very slowly for Gillian, and she could hardly keep her excitement in check. She was hoping Kyle would stop and talk to her about his plans. She didn't see him that day except during lunch when he was too busy with one of the other staff members to talk.

By the time she had finished the evening meal, she had almost given up seeing him before the next day. Just as she was about to start back to her cabin, Kyle met her at the door of the kitchen.

"Good evening, Gillian."

"Hi, Kyle."

"You haven't changed your mind about tomorrow, have you?" Kyle asked with a grin.

"I wouldn't miss it for the world," answered Gillian enthusiastically.

"We'll need to leave pretty early," he warned.

"That's all right."

"How does five-thirty sound?"

"Fine. The earlier the better," she answered without wincing.

"I'll stop by your cabin at a quarter after. Are you quite sure you'll be ready?"

"Positive."

"See you tomorrow, then," Kyle called over his shoulder as he turned to walk away. Gillian stood for a few minutes looking after him. He looked particularly handsome tonight, she noticed.

On her way back to her cabin, Gillian thought about what might happen the next day. She had to admit she was at least a little afraid since she had never been canoeing before, but she was sure Kyle would watch out for her.

The most exciting part was that she would spend the whole day alone with Kyle. He had been in her thoughts a great deal lately. She only hoped he thought as much of her.

That night Gillian read more of her Bible and then went to sleep early. She would need to get up before dawn to be ready when Kyle arrived, and she wanted to be alert while she was learning to canoe. Sleep seemed to come slowly, but her thoughts were on pleasant things when she finally drifted off.

The next morning Gillian woke much earlier than she had intended. She tried to fall back to sleep, but the anticipation made her even more wakeful while she lay and thought about her day.

Eventually her excitement won out and she decided to get up and dress. Kyle would not be there for at least an hour, so she worked at filling the time as best she could.

After reading the first line in a new book several times, she tossed it into a corner and looked for something else to do. Absentmindedly, she picked up her Bible and once more flipped through the pages.

She had not had it opened for long when one of the verses seemed to jump out at her from the page. It read, "There is no one righteous, not even one; there is no one who understands, no one who seeks God. All have turned away, they have together become worthless; there is no one who does good, not even one."

For some reason, these words seemed to burn themselves into Gillian's heart. This statement sounded so desperate. Did it include Jake? Could he have missed reading this? How could she ever tell him? He would be devastated.

Gillian sat for a long time, thinking through this dilemma. Before she realized how long she had spent, she heard a knock on the door and rushed to open it. Kyle stood in front of her, smiling. The sun was just beginning to rise on the edge of the horizon. She glimpsed at it over Kyle's shoulder as its first rays made his blond hair shine.

"Are you ready to go?"

"Yes," was all that Gillian could answer.

Kyle closed the door behind them as they started down the path toward the docks. Silence seemed to hang in the morning mist—almost a reverence for the solitude of the early hour. Gillian's thoughts leapt ahead to the trip. Would Kyle give her some sign today of how he felt about her?

When they reached the dock, Kyle pulled a tarp off a canoe rocking gently in the water by the first pier. Gillian was told how to board the canoe and given a few quick safety pointers. Then Kyle picked up a nearby paddle and showed her the different strokes she would need to know. After her brief lesson, they climbed into the canoe.

Gillian's heart fluttered as Kyle pushed the canoe away from the dock and she felt the movement of the water beneath them. The paddle felt strange, and she struggled to make it move in the patterns she had been coached to use.

"Don't try so hard," Kyle's voice spoke gently from behind her.

She took a deep breath and then tried again slowly. It worked and Gillian found she could maneuver it quite well. In no time they were gliding past the other boats and out into the slow-moving river before them.

From her vantage point in the front of the canoe, Gillian could see everything that slipped by them. As she looked at the water streaming from the point of the bow, she felt they were moving far too speedily. A quick glance at the banks on either side of them reassured her that it was not true. The canoe moved deliberately yet gracefully down the center of the river.

Before long, the sun rose above the tips of the trees, taking the morning chill from the air. It played across the surface of the water and brought the sound of birds from the forest edge.

"It's getting warm," Kyle called suddenly from behind her.

Startled by the unexpected voice, Gillian turned quickly to look back at him and felt a sudden lurch from the canoe beneath her. Before she realized what was happening, the cold water rushed over her head and she could feel herself sinking into its depths. Instinctively she fought against the water and soon surfaced beside the overturned canoe. She could hear Kyle's laughter.

"I'll know not to call out before warning you first," he said with a wide grin on his face, his eyes dancing merrily.

"I'm sorry!" Gillian cried out breathlessly as soon as she could talk.

"It's okay," Kyle answered, still smiling even though water streamed from his hair and down his face. "I expected it. Most people tip a canoe their first time out. It's not going to be easy getting her right side up again. We're out pretty deep."

They tried several times to right the overturned canoe, but it was no use. In the end they had to swim to shore, pushing the canoe along in front of them.

Together they slid the craft onto the bank, and Kyle checked to make sure none of the cargo they were carrying had gotten wet. He had tied it all securely to the canoe in waterproof bags because he feared this very thing might happen. Everything was safe and dry. Then he turned to Gillian.

"Do you have anything else to wear that's dry?"

"I'm afraid not," she answered, feeling very foolish in her dripping clothes.

"I have another shirt, but you'll have to wear wet jeans for a while," he said sympathetically.

"What will you wear, then?"

"I have another pair of pants along, and I don't need to wear a shirt," he answered, going to retrieve his shirt from the waterproof duffel bag in the canoe.

Gillian humbly took Kyle's shirt and walked into the

bushes to change into it. The shirt fit her poorly. She could roll up the sleeves, but the shoulders drooped. The rest of it gave her ample room, but it was better than wearing her own wet shirt.

Gillian walked quietly back to the canoe and watched Kyle push it out into the shallow water once again. A deep scar on his side caught her eye as he turned back to her.

"Kyle," she asked, her voice filled with concern, "how did you get that nasty scar?"

"This?" returned Kyle lightly. "It's just from an operation I had a year or two back. Nothing serious." Gillian winced at the thought but said nothing more.

Before long, they set out again. Gillian was determined to be more careful this time.

The sun swung higher into the sky and the canoe crossed the lake that the stream had emptied into. On the other side of the lake, they entered another stream and continued.

Gillian heard Kyle cough and then cough again. "He must be getting a cold from that dunking this morning," she concluded pitifully, then thought she heard him cautiously whisper her name.

Uncertain of whether she was imagining it, she chose to ignore the sound. Then she heard it again.

When she turned around, she saw Kyle grinning mischievously.

"I wanted to tell you that it's time to stop for lunch, but I didn't want to startle you into another mishap."

Gillian's face turned red as she felt her anger rise. But when she saw his mustache quivering, she relaxed.

Kyle, you're such a child sometimes, she wanted to say, but she didn't want to offend him. Deep inside she knew she didn't want him to change, either.

They paddled over toward a clearing on the bank and Gillian jumped out into the shallow water just before the bottom of the canoe grated against the sand and rocks beneath. She was surprised how stiff her legs had become with only half a day of canoeing.

The sandwiches were delicious, especially after the exercise of the morning and the fresh air, which seemed to make her even hungrier than usual. At first they ate in silence, deep in their own thoughts. As her mind drifted, Gillian remembered her dilemma of the morning and decided to ask Kyle about it.

"Kyle," she began timidly, "do you mind if I ask you a question?"

"Not at all. Fire away."

"Well, this morning I was reading the Bible Jake gave me. I don't understand something it said."

Kyle's head popped up from his apple and he seemed to get a hopeful look in his eye. Gillian chose to ignore it and continued.

"The verse said something about every person on earth having sinned and that nobody is even trying to know God. I don't remember how it was put, but it was something to that effect." At Kyle's nod of recognition, she went on. "What I don't understand is, if no one is trying to get close to God, how can there be any Christians at all? I mean, does that mean that not even the Christians are really trying to live for Him? The verse said that not one of them is good."

Kyle lowered his apple and thought for a moment, then answered slowly, "I believe what the verse means is that when the first people sinned for the first time they deliberately chose to leave the close relationship with God which they had enjoyed. Now every person that is born has a part of him that strives to keep away from God. The Bible says that when Jesus Christ came down to earth as a man and died for our sins, He made it possible for us to be reinstated into God's favor. Because of what He did, we have been offered a chance to have the privilege of calling ourselves

Christians. Do you understand what I'm trying to say?"

"I think I do," Gillian answered thoughtfully. "My sins are what is keeping God from being able to get close to me." She paused, uncertain of how to continue.

"He's sure been trying, Kyle," she admitted candidly. "It seems like every person I've talked to lately has taught me some new part of what being a Christian is. Jake has done a lot and Aunt Lucy made it seem so simple. Why can't I just accept it?"

"There is something else you need to know, Gillian," Kyle answered, looking directly into her eyes. "Satan is real too, and he is doing his best to work against what God is doing in your life. He doesn't want to lose you."

"I didn't know he ever had me!" Gillian exclaimed, repulsed by the thought.

"He's terribly clever in that way. He convinces us that we're really not all that bad, but the Bible says that the only way we can escape from Satan's grasp is to use the power Jesus made available to us on the cross. When Christ releases us from sin, we're also released from the devil's hold on us. We still have to resist him from time to time, but as we claim victory in Jesus, Satan loses the control he once had."

Gillian thought to herself for a moment and then slowly got to her feet. "I know you're in a hurry to get downriver, Kyle," she said deliberately, "so we'd better get started again."

Kyle sat for just a moment longer and watched her. The look of hopefulness in his eye wavered but did not disappear. At last he rose and began to reload the canoe as Gillian cleared away the remains of their lunch.

During the remainder of the canoe trip, the two chatted amiably about light topics, and the time seemed to fly past. Before long the sun was beginning to set and the lights in the few cabins they passed were being turned on.

"We're almost there," Kyle called. "Just around this next bend we should see the truck waiting for us."

The canoe glided slowly around the bend and Gillian caught sight of a bridge that bent easily across the river. The truck sat quietly off to the side of the road to the left of the bridge.

"I don't see anyone. Isn't somebody going to meet us?" Gillian called back to Kyle.

"No, we leave the canoe on the bank and drive the truck back to camp. They'll pick the canoe up in the morning."

The canoe landed on the shore with a slight bump, and Gillian climbed out for the last time. Kyle pulled it up onto the shore and covered it with a tarp, then joined Gillian and helped carry their day's supplies up to the waiting truck.

"Why didn't the men just drive the truck up to camp to get whatever cargo we are carrying instead of our going to all the trouble of leaving it here in the canoe?" Gillian asked innocently.

Kyle reached for the truck door and opened it before he answered, "Because I wouldn't have been able to spend the day teaching you to canoe then, would I?"

Gillian's eyes widened and she climbed quickly into the cab to hide her surprise.

The ride home was quiet but very pleasant.

13

$\mathcal{G}$illian lay in bed thinking for a long time that night. She had learned so many things in one day that it made her head spin. She had enjoyed learning to canoe and was still on a high because of the activity, but her thoughts were not centered on that. She also thought about Kyle. The words he had spoken to her just as they were climbing into the truck had engraved themselves in her mind. Had Kyle really gone out of his way to spend time with her?

The thought that plagued her the most, however, was the meaning of the verses Kyle had explained. She had never pictured herself as an evil person, but she supposed in light of what the verse had said, she was. She certainly hadn't given God much thought before she had come to this camp.

Maybe that's what the verse had meant. That she was one of the unrighteous people who hadn't felt the need for God in her life. Kyle had said that since Christ had died on the cross, she could be given the freedom He had intended for her in the first place. He would try to speak to her even though she hadn't tried to reach out to Him first.

It was all so confusing, yet somehow it seemed to make more sense as she learned each new truth. Tomorrow she would talk to Jake, but for tonight she really needed some sleep.

No matter how much she tried to push the thoughts away, they persisted. Finally, she admitted to herself that she needed to make some kind of decision that night.

Gillian reached out slowly and turned on the light. The Bible lay on the table and she picked it up reverently. It had sparked questions for her before; perhaps it would also be a good place to look for answers.

She flipped the pages open carefully and began to read, at first disappointed that she couldn't understand what she read. But it didn't take her long to find a verse that spoke directly to her. It said, "Behold, I stand at the door and knock. If any man should hear my voice and will open the door, I will come in."

Gillian sat quietly for a moment, fingering the pages. Could she make such a big decision without even talking to someone first? That wasn't entirely true, though. She had talked to lots of people. First Jake, then Kyle, and then Aunt Lucy. Aunt Lucy's words came back to her now. She remembered that all a person had to do was to accept what Christ had proclaimed to be true. The Bible was clear enough.

Without a moment's hesitation, Gillian flipped back the covers and sat on the edge of the bed, holding on to the Bible tightly. The words came slowly and painstakingly at first; then they began to tumble out.

"God, I'm not sure how to talk to you, but I really think I want to try now. I've been avoiding you for so long and I realize now that it's because I'm a sinner. I don't want to be. What I really want is to ask you to take my sins away. Kyle said you could do that because you died on the cross." For a moment Gillian paused, thinking about the weight of those simple words. "I want to thank you for that. I still don't understand why you did, but I'll try to just accept it and not question your reasons. Please help me to live the way that a follower of Jesus should. I want you to be happy with me."

As Gillian lay down, she felt different—as if she were standing in God's pleasure instead of under His judgment. *It's as if I'm truly alive,* she thought.

She pulled up the covers and turned off the light. The

bed seemed softer and the dark much more comfortable. She stretched her toes far into the folds of the blankets and breathed in deeply. If what she was feeling was Christianity, she decided she liked it.

In no time at all she fell asleep, dreaming of pleasant things and waking very refreshed.

The next morning she whistled as she walked down the path to the shower. The whole world seemed to know the tune and blend right in with it. Every bird joined in, along with the morning breeze and the rustling branches, while the sun smiled more brilliantly than she remembered it doing before. The day was truly glorious.

"Gillian," a voice called from behind her, "wait for me."

Sharon came scurrying up the path, and Gillian stepped aside to wait, a big grin spreading across her face.

"Ask me why I'm so happy this morning, Sharon," Gillian prodded.

"Why?" Sharon answered, still trying to catch her breath.

"Because I made a very big decision last night," she answered elusively.

"You're going to run for prime minister," responded Sharon with light sarcasm.

"No, I—" suddenly Gillian couldn't find the right words.

"You're what?" Sharon urged.

"I'm a Christian," she answered awkwardly.

Sharon knew what to do. "Oh, Gillian, I'm so happy!" she exclaimed and grabbed her in a fierce hug. "Tell me all about it."

Gillian related the past events to Sharon as they walked down the path together. Sharon's step took on a bounce almost as light as Gillian's, and neither could stop smiling.

The day went quickly and Gillian took every opportunity she could to share her newly found faith with those around her. Almost everyone was excited for her, and her confidence grew by leaps and bounds. The only setback she had was at lunch when she saw Randy.

"Why are you so chipper today?" he asked.

"Because I've finally made a decision to be a Christian," Gillian answered candidly.

"Oh," was all he said, but his face gave the impression he wasn't very excited about it. Gillian had no idea that to Randy that meant he had lost out in the race for her, but his disappointed look stole some of her pleasure.

That evening at vespers, Jake asked Gillian to give the good news to everyone who was there. Although somewhat shy, she freely gave a recount of her past few weeks. Everyone listened intently and then clapped when she finished. She found herself smiling. It was wonderful to have such support.

When the meeting was over, Gillian rose to leave, but it was no simple process that night. People she didn't even know well came to hug and encourage her. She was told over and over how wonderful it was that she had made the right decision.

Suddenly strong arms encircled her. Confused, she looked up and saw Kyle's face smiling down at her. His mustache was drawn up in a wide smile, but there was an unexpected tear in his eye.

"I was so glad to hear it," Kyle smiled happily.

Gillian smiled back and he slowly released her. For a moment he looked deeply into her eyes and then began to speak quietly.

Before she could catch Kyle's words, she felt herself being pulled away from him by another group of well-wishers. When she finally got a chance to look around, he was gone.

By the time Gillian arrived at her cabin, it was very late. She tossed herself down on the bed and breathed in deeply. It had been a good day—a very good day—but it had completely worn her out. Maybe tomorrow things would settle back into their old familiar pattern.

14

"*G*illian," a voice broke into her deep sleep.

"Gillian, are you awake?" it called again from outside her door.

Gillian rose hurriedly and threw on her robe.

"Who is it?" she answered.

"It's Kyle. Sorry to wake you, but I'd like to talk with you and I have to be at the stables soon."

"Just a minute," Gillian responded, scrambling into her clothes and quickly brushing out the tangles from her hair.

"This is a crazy time to want to talk," Gillian scolded Kyle with a laugh as she closed the door behind her.

"I'm truly sorry," answered Kyle, "but I couldn't bear the thought of waiting until tonight."

"What's so important?"

"I just wanted to talk for a bit, that's all," he said, backing down from his original sincerity.

Gillian smiled at his sudden nonchalance but decided to play along. He had to have a better reason than that for waking her up so early.

"Would you like to go for a walk?" Kyle asked casually.

"Sure, but let me get a jacket. The morning is too cool for just a shirt."

The two strolled quietly down the path that led to the lake and stood in silence, watching the brilliant sunrise.

"I was so glad to hear you were doing so much serious thinking about God these last few weeks," Kyle said, breaking the spell.

"It seems like it was all planned out so well," Gillian answered thoughtfully. "I mean, everything fit together to help me understand the whole picture like I never have before. It's just as if God has been planning every move I've made lately."

"He has."

"I'm so glad He made the effort to reach me. It just amazes me that God would work so hard to get my attention."

"He's done that for all of us, in different ways. We should all feel grateful. In my case, He gave me a loving Christian family and a wonderful church. Sometimes it didn't seem like all of that would be enough to keep me close to Him. I had a few very unfortunate years I'd like nothing better than to erase. I suppose God uses these experiences to test us. He wants to see if we really intend to serve Him with our whole hearts."

Kyle could not stay much longer. People began to walk by on their way to their various tasks, and he felt he too should be at his job.

"I wish we could talk more right now. I just wanted you to know that your decision was—well, important to me. A real answer to prayer," Kyle finally said awkwardly. As he spoke he looked nervously from the lake to Mount Judas, avoiding Gillian's questioning eyes. "Will I see you later today?" he asked, at last meeting her gaze.

"Sure, I'll stop by. Sharon's in the kitchen so it's my day off."

"I didn't realize that. Why don't you come down to the stables and give me a hand?"

"I'd like that. Just give me a chance to shower and finish up some things I have to do here, and I'll be there."

Kyle walked off down the path whistling, and Gillian scurried back to her cabin to rush through her morning duties. In no time at all she was running down the path toward the stables.

The morning was filled with a variety of activities. Kyle advised Gillian not to try cleaning a stall, but she insisted. Though the experience was not pleasant, she was proud that she had done it anyway.

Wanting something a little easier to handle, Gillian next groomed some of the horses. When she was finished with them, they shone in the morning light and whinnied their thanks loudly as they munched on the grain in front of them.

Kyle followed her down the line of horses, checking hooves for lodged stones and paying special attention to certain horses that had ailments.

"Do you do this every morning?" Gillian asked cheerfully.

"Yes, we do. It's important to take very good care of the animals. They're much more content with a rider on their back if they don't have a stone in their shoe or a burr in their saddle."

"I guess that makes sense."

When Gillian came to the colt she had met when he was a day old, she was very startled. The little wobbly baby had grown into a well-developed bundle of energy. Kyle said the colt was gentle enough for her to go into the stall and pet him, so she climbed over the rails.

The smell of musty hay hung heavily in the air around her since the stall was completely closed in. The colt kicked up his heels when he saw Gillian and, being badly spoiled by the stable hands, trotted over expecting a treat. Gillian tousled the fuzzy hair between his ears and stroked his neck tenderly. A wet nose bumped into her arm and sniffed at her pockets. When the colt didn't find what he was searching for, he began to chew on Gillian's shirttail instead, as if that would make up for the lack of something sweeter. Gillian couldn't help but giggle at him.

"What's his name?" Gillian called over her shoulder and was startled by Kyle's voice nearby.

"His name is Solomon."

"I didn't know you were watching," Gillian responded, turning to face him. "Is he yours?"

"Yes," came the proud reply, "and he's going to be a fine stallion someday."

Gillian turned back to the little animal now pulling at her shoelaces. "So you're going to be a fine stallion some-day," she whispered. "Then you'd better learn not to chew on people's clothes. It's all right from a little guy like you, but when you're big and strong, it won't be so funny." The colt looked up at her innocently and she giggled, "No, it won't be funny at all."

The colt sneezed out a nod and Gillian laughed harder. As she turned to leave, she gave him one last pat on the nose.

"He's beautiful," she said to Kyle as she crawled out over the bars of the gate.

"He'll be one of the best horses I've ever owned," Kyle answered.

Just then Randy returned with a group of riders he had taken out. They were all joking and laughing, and it made Gillian proud to be a member of the staff. She hurried off with Kyle to get the stalls ready for the returning horses.

Randy scowled when he saw the two of them together. It wasn't fair. He had always felt strongly for Gillian and, until she announced her decision to fall in with Kyle and the others in their beliefs, he had thought it was just a matter of time before she shared his feelings.

Kyle stepped out of the stall to find the pitchfork, and Randy followed closely behind him.

"You're not wasting any time, are you?" he accused Kyle.

"What are you talking about?" Kyle returned patiently.

"You know exactly what I mean. Now that you have brainwashed Gillian into believing like you do, you think it's all right to consider her 'available.' And you don't even know if she's serious about it or not."

"How's that?" Kyle deliberately sounded unconvinced.

"She decided—what?—two days ago. That's not much time to prove she's serious, is it? Maybe in a couple more days she'll change her mind again." The words began to find their target, and Randy continued. "And how do you know that she didn't just pretend to give in—for your sake? Maybe she knew how you felt and thought that lying would be worth it."

Kyle set down the bale he was lifting and turned to face Randy fully. "For someone who thinks he has so many feelings for Gillian, you certainly have a low opinion of her. First you say she might be unstable in her beliefs, and then you accuse her of being a liar. So why are you fighting so hard? Could it be that you don't really believe any of those things yourself?"

Randy glared back at Kyle and then spun sharply on his heel, striding away with angry steps. Kyle ran a quick hand through his hair as he watched Randy leave, his mind refusing to dismiss the accusations as quickly as his words had. Maybe he was being hasty. Gillian had so recently become a Christian. Perhaps he should wait until he was certain about her commitment. He knew well enough that there were many levels of Christian zeal. There were some who were content to simply use the name and forget the responsibilities that came with it. How could he know what Gillian's intentions were?

There was a slight droop in his shoulders as he lifted the bale and hefted it over to the stalls. The excitement he had felt only moments ago seemed to drain from him, leaving a void. With careful effort he masked his heavy thoughts and acted, as much as possible, like his usual self. He tried inconspicuously to keep his distance from Gillian. If it was best that he wait, then wait he would.

By lunchtime, Gillian had learned a great deal about the care of a horse. As she and Kyle walked back to the dining hall, she asked many more questions and Kyle was more than willing to answer all of them. Her interest in his work made him feel satisfied with it himself.

After lunch Gillian took a book from her cabin and sat by the lake to read. She spent a lazy afternoon watching the flocks of birds gather on the lake.

Fall was coming on the camp. She pulled her jacket more tightly around her at the thought. The mountainsides held patches of yellow where the trees were changing color. Gillian missed the array of colors at home where the trees exploded into a brilliance of many hues at the change of weather, but she couldn't deny the beauty she saw here. During the morning, the mountains around her were clear blue, but in the evening they stood purple against the orange sky. The sky itself was always clear and when rain did fall, it seemed to make the world even more alive and dynamic as it left its scattered gems of raindrops sparkling on the grass and trees.

Kate had told her that all too soon the snow would come. Then the camp's business would gradually slow during winter. There would be few men who dared to hunt in the snow-covered forest and even fewer who wanted to fish where they had to first chop a hole through the ice. It was because of this that Kate said winter was a very relaxing time for the staff. Some of them returned to their farms for the season, but for those who stayed, the days were fulfilling. They had less responsibility and more time to spend together enjoying the company of friends. There would be skiing trips and snow fights, snowmobile races along the river, and popcorn around the fire in the dining hall. Gillian could hardly wait.

The cold wind pushed her back to her cabin, where she lay on the bed writing letters home. As she chewed on the pencil wondering how she could put her feelings into words, she realized how distant she felt from her friends and family. Krystal had always hated the outdoors. She was much more content to watch television and play quiet games than to get out and enjoy the sunshine. Gillian's mother's idea of spending time with nature was to plant a new rosebush in her immense garden. Gillian loved her mother's garden, but somehow it lacked the spontaneity that God had weaved into His.

Her father was the only member of her family who fully appreciated the wilderness. He had grown up in the mountains of northern British Columbia and had learned much about life there. It was not until he had met Gillian's mother that he had ever thought of leaving his home. His plans to return someday had been thwarted by the events of the passing years, and Gillian knew he would probably never realize his dream. It was sad, but that was life.

The letters were written slowly and painfully, as if to strangers. Gillian did not like the feeling, but she found she couldn't shake it. Her life had changed a great deal over the summer months and, although she would often think about what she had left behind, she knew she could never truly leave this place. Perhaps she would move to a city or town close by, but she was a victim to the spell cast by the mountains, and they claimed her as their own.

15

$\mathcal{T}$he next day settled back into routine. People smiled at Gillian often, but no one mentioned her decision to follow Christ. She spent most of her day in the kitchen making plans for the coming week and doing some special baking she had wanted to do for a while.

Late in the day, Kate stopped by and greeted her warmly.

"Gillian," she said, smiling broadly, "John had a wonderful idea the other day. His family is having a reunion on Vancouver Island next week and we're expected to go. I'm usually pretty bored when we go, but you know how it is. I have to show up and at least smile at everyone for a day. It's not that I don't like his relatives; they just don't go out of their way to include me, so I'm usually left on the outside.

"Anyway, John suggested I take you and Sharon with me and spend some time at Long Beach while he visits with the family. It will only be for four days, and I'm sure we'd have a good time. What do you say?"

Gillian wanted to go very badly, but she had some misgivings. "Wouldn't that leave the kitchen without anyone in charge?"

"Yes, but it will be Monday through Thursday of next week. I went over our guest list for those days, and we have only about ten men. Tim could handle it easily."

Gillian was more than willing to be talked into the trip and ran to call Sharon. Sharon too was excited and the three made plans for their short vacation.

When Monday morning burst out in a shower of sunshine, Gillian's spirits soared. They loaded John's car and jumped inside, each of them looking forward to the time ahead.

During the long ride, they chatted about the events of the past week and the plans for the long fall months ahead. Kate and John remarked about the increased number of campers, setting a record for that year, and Sharon, after casting a mischievous look in Gillian's direction, promptly asked for a raise.

Away from all reminders of the work at camp, Gillian found it easy to forget each of their positions and simply see them as friends. It was good to feel comfortable with them at last. By the time they began their descent toward the ocean, Gillian had completely forgotten her previous difficulties.

As they approached Vancouver, conversation waned as John pointed out various interesting buildings on the skyline for Gillian's benefit. At last she got her first view of the ocean as they drove over the crest of a long hill.

The hill fell sharply to the water's edge, with trees and houses lining its slopes. Gillian looked out across the water and watched the boats floating slowly down the broad strait.

"We're almost there," Kate called eagerly. "I can see the ferry just pulling into the dock. John, you'd better hurry or we'll miss it."

"Don't get excited, Kate," John answered calmly. "We have plenty of time to get there before the ferry leaves. They have to unload first, and we'll be there before they even begin loading."

Gillian had not realized that they would be traveling in a ferry across to Vancouver Island. The idea appealed to her, and she silently urged John to hurry.

They arrived at the gate and Kate asked the man working in the booth beside it if he thought they would be able to board the docked ferry. He assured her they were on time, and John smiled victoriously at Kate. Kate returned his look with a playful punch in the arm, and they moved ahead to join the line of cars in front of them.

When Gillian saw the cars ahead, snaking their way across the parking lot, it reminded her of the lines she had so often waited in to go on rides at amusement parks. This line moved no more quickly. The cars inched along toward the ship, stopping and starting and filling the air with their fumes.

At last they moved close enough to the ferry to watch the cars in front of them board. The ship opened into a huge garagelike room that already held row upon row of crowded cars. A heavy ramp reached from the dock to the ferry and the cars edged slowly and carefully up it until they were across the makeshift bridge and securely on the boat.

Gillian felt a chill run down her spine as John drove the car easily onto the ramp. As the car moved forward, the dock seemed to fall away beneath her and she felt her stomach fall with it. The car in front of them stopped short and John braked quickly to avoid hitting it. Gillian swallowed hard and tried to shut out the sound of the waves smashing against the beams far beneath them. At last they began to move again.

When they reached the parking area, several men directed the cars to where they were to park. John skillfully maneuvered the car close against the others. Then they all jumped out, hurrying to get away from the smell of exhaust heavily permeating the air. Gillian followed the others to a central stairwell leading to the upper decks.

Arriving back up in the fresh, cold air, Gillian felt her stamina return, and they huddled near the rail to watch the ship depart from the dock. Already cars were waiting for the next ferry, and Gillian felt relieved that they were not among them.

The ride was much longer than Gillian expected it to be. The boat rocked gently as it lumbered across the water with its burdensome cargo, and a cold, wet wind began to whip across the deck.

"Let's find a seat inside before they're all taken," Kate suggested.

"I think I'd like to stay out here and watch the other boats," Sharon answered. "I don't get to see the ocean very often anymore."

Gillian decided to stay with Sharon, and John and Kate went inside.

"I've never been on a ferry before," Gillian commented simply.

"I used to ride it all the time," Sharon responded. "I lived in Nanaimo for most of my life."

"Where's Nanaimo?" Gillian asked.

"It's on Vancouver Island," answered Sharon.

Gillian felt silly at her lack of knowledge, but Sharon soon put her at ease. "Nanaimo is not nearly as well known as Vancouver. It's not on the mainland, but it's close enough to feel set apart from the crowds without being completely secluded. I have a lot of good memories of living there."

As the boats passed on either side of the ferry making its way across the wide strait, Gillian watched them thoughtfully. It seemed that each boat told a story and had somehow acquired a personality. The small fishing boat bobbing against the horizon was a relic of days gone by, set aside and forgotten by a speedily changing world. The slender speedboat playing across the ferry's wake was the young generation, laughing at tradition and always searching for what was new and untried.

"My brother had a boat when I was young," Sharon mused dreamily. "It was a sailboat he and my grandfather built, and it was a beauty. My brother used to race it and won most of the time." Then her tone changed.

"When he moved to the States for college, he had to sell his boat to help pay for tuition. I'll never forget how he looked that day. He walked into the house and just stood there with his head hung low. I couldn't stand it and ran to my room and cried. He came and told me that it wasn't so bad, and that he'd build another one someday, but I knew he wouldn't. Two years later Grandpa died. Alex won't ever be able to build another boat without him. I still feel like crying when I think about it."

The speedboat tired of its play and moved on to find some other means of entertainment. Without a word, Sharon turned to walk farther along the deck, and Gillian stood alone, thinking.

The ferry docked on Vancouver Island and the group moved slowly back to their cars. As the engines started up, the noise and fumes were difficult to bear. The cars moved forward toward the other end of the ferry and disembarked slowly.

When they were once more on the open road, heading into Nanaimo, Sharon pointed out the different buildings and landmarks familiar to her. Gillian smiled at her excited chatter and was glad she had cheered up. Memories could be cruel at times.

Before long they were moving out of the city into the country. There were many trees, most of them evergreens that hid all views of the ocean, making it easy for Gillian to forget she was on an island.

"We're going to drop you off at Long Beach while Kate and I run over to the reunion and see the relatives," John announced. "We won't be long. It's going to be held only thirteen miles farther up the coast at my uncle's beach house."

Sharon and Gillian grew very excited when they pulled

into the beach parking lot. They still couldn't see the water, but they could smell it in the chilly air.

"I'll race you to the shore," Sharon cried, grabbing her jacket and running ahead without waiting for Gillian to answer. Gillian chased her over a small ridge where they both stopped short on the crest of a steep hill. Before them lay the ocean, stretching out for miles and miles. The strait lying between Vancouver Island and the mainland seemed at first to be the ocean, but they knew it wasn't. Now they gazed in awe across the waters that they knew spread all the way to the banks of Japan.

"Let's go," Sharon said breathlessly and finished her descent down the tree-covered hill.

"What are we going to do first?" Gillian asked when they reached the sandy shore.

"See those rocks?" Sharon pointed out. "Let's go out there."

The two ran toward the rocks and carelessly climbed over them, discovering sea anemone, starfish, and a multitude of barnacles. For Gillian, all the sights were new, but Sharon took pride in explaining each one. Together they wandered farther down the beach.

It was not long before John and Kate returned and added to the fun. John had brought a frisbee, and they started a game of keep-away. The afternoon passed quickly and the sun began to set long before any of them were ready to leave.

"Look at the sunset," Kate called breathlessly. "It's beautiful!"

They all flopped down on the sand in exhaustion, listening to the soft rise and fall of the waves washing the sandy beach.

"It seems as if it goes on forever!" Gillian exclaimed with a sigh. "The ocean is just so big."

The next two days sped by and before long they were

once again on the ferry, gliding toward the mainland.

"I'm glad we went," Sharon whispered to Gillian as they leaned over the rail of the ship.

"I guess you really must have missed the ocean since you moved inland."

"Yes," Sharon replied, "but mostly I'm glad I got a chance to get to know you even better. You're a good friend, Gillian."

Gillian smiled back. As they looked out over the water, her heart whispered, *Thank you, God.*

16

Weeks went by and Gillian fell into a pleasant routine. During the day she was busy in the kitchen, but her free time was spent helping Kyle at the stables. Although she was frustrated at times because Kyle was so distant, she continued to search him out, hoping for some sign of encouragement from him. In the meantime, she became completely at ease around the horses and was treated with respect by the campers, some of whom were still learning the basics of riding. She spent her evenings visiting Kate, walking with Jake, or playing chess with Kyle. She didn't ever win when she played chess, but she enjoyed his company, and Kyle didn't seem to mind the extra boost that playing with Gillian gave to his ego.

One day while she was at the stables brushing the horses down after a long ride, she heard a commotion outside and ran to explore. As she turned the corner of the building, she saw a man lying on the ground, a cloud of dust hovering over him.

"What on earth were you doing?" Randy was shouting.

The man crawled stiffly to his feet and grinned awkwardly. "I saw that in a movie once and it looked easy enough."

"Well, it's not!" Randy snapped. "Our horses are not trained to have someone stand on their backs, and you certainly don't have the skill either. I'd appreciate it if you'd just stick to learning how to ride sitting down."

Randy stormed off to help the other riders and to cool down, leaving the tall man standing humbly on his own. He stooped over, picked up his black felt cowboy hat, and brushed at the dirt clinging to its bright red feathers. The man wore a denim jacket and leather riding chaps.

Gillian went quickly to ask him if he was hurt, and he took the opportunity to use his well-practiced speech on her. "Howdy, ma'am," he tried to drawl. "Are you one of them there—whatcha call—wranglers?"

"I'm just helping a friend," Gillian answered, trying not to laugh at the poor man. "Is this your first riding lesson?"

"Yes'm," the man answered slowly, as if calculating every word. "I'm here to learn to be a cowpoke and tame some doggies."

"You'd better get back to the lesson, Mr.—" Gillian didn't know his name.

"Name's Roscoe, ma'am," the man swaggered, "Gilbert Floyd Roscoe, and if I can ever be of service to ya, jest holler."

Gillian humored him with a nod and then walked back to the stables where she fell against the rails laughing.

After some time, Randy came muttering into the building and slammed his fist against a post. "That man infuriates me," he muttered angrily. "He's trying to be some old western movie hero, and I don't think he can even tie his own shoe. If he doesn't kill himself trying something stupid before he leaves, I'll be surprised."

"Do you really think he'll get hurt?" Gillian asked, suddenly very concerned.

"Probably not, I guess, but we'll have to watch him pretty close. He's trying to be John Wayne, but he's really worse than all three Stooges."

Gillian thought for a moment and then sighed. There had never been anyone seriously hurt while she was at the camp and the thought scared her. It was true that there were many ways a person could have an accident, but she had dared to hope that none of these would happen here.

She walked slowly back to the kitchen in a pensive mood. If there was something she could do to keep Gilbert Roscoe from hurting himself, she decided she'd better do it. She knew she served a God of love, so it was important that she learn to love others. Gilbert certainly needed someone to take care of him.

Perhaps she would see him at supper that night. She had the next day off and could offer to show him around— just to supervise him for a while.

Gilbert was easy to find at supper. He was loud and awkward, but Gillian tactfully made arrangements to "help him get acquainted with the wilderness" the next morning. She wasn't sure just what she was going to do with him, but she would think of something.

The next morning Gillian was wrenched from sleep by a loud banging on her cabin door. When she rose and called to the intruder, she recognized Gilbert's voice shouting back, "Mornin'. Why don't ya come on out and fry us up some griddle cakes and we'll start the day out right."

Gillian stumbled back to her bedroom and cringed when she looked at her clock. It was five-thirty in the morning and it was her day off. How could Gilbert be so inconsiderate? "This isn't going to be easy," she muttered to herself.

She tried to act perky and alert as she whipped the batter and poured pancake after pancake onto the griddle. Gilbert may not be able to do much else, but he certainly could fit stacks of pancakes into his tall, skinny frame.

After three cups of coffee, Gillian found she could finally think clearly and asked Gilbert if he had wanted to see anything special.

"I want to go bear hunting," he answered quickly, and immediately Gillian was sorry she had asked.

"We can't hunt bear today," Gillian answered evenly. "They're not in season."

Gilbert's face fell and he shook his head slowly. "They told me I could do some hunting while I was here. That's what I wanted most of all."

"You can go hunting," Gillian added quickly, "but you'd have to hunt ducks, and I couldn't take you. I don't even know how to load a gun, much less how to shoot the thing."

"Can you take me to the people who can teach me?"

Gillian paused for a moment and remembered Randy's fateful words, "Wouldn't you like to go fishing instead?"

"Daniel Boone did not become famous for fishing," Gilbert answered with injured pride. "I want to hunt."

Gillian gave in against her better judgment and escorted Gilbert down to the riflery range. The camp was just beginning to stir, and when they saw the instructor at the practice range, Gillian introduced Gilbert to him.

"Murray," Gillian said formally, "this is Gilbert Roscoe and he would like to learn to shoot a gun."

"Have you ever had any experience with guns before, Mr. Roscoe?" Murray asked routinely.

"No," Gilbert answered, "but I saw lots of movies, so I know I can do it."

"It's not as easy to learn as it is to watch in a movie," Murray answered patiently, "It takes a lot of practice."

"I'm sure I can do it," Gilbert responded quickly.

Gillian followed Gilbert and Murray to the practice range, where Murray unlocked the booth holding the guns owned by the camp. Several other men had already arrived and dotted the field as they set up for practice.

"All right," said Murray, picking up a nearby .22. "The first thing you need to know is that a gun is not a toy. It is a weapon and should never be handled carelessly or by unsupervised beginners."

Murray placed the small gun in Gilbert's hands, who promptly swung it toward a target.

"Put that down!" Murray shouted. "There are half a dozen men out there still putting up targets, and if that gun had been loaded you probably would have hit one. Always keep a gun pointed at the ground beside you until you are ready to shoot."

Gilbert swung the gun down to his side, knocking against the row of rifles neatly leaned against a rack beside him. With a loud crash, they fell to the ground like dominoes.

"Mr. Roscoe!" Murray burst out, rapidly losing his cool, "you've got to be careful. Do you understand that?"

"Of course," Gilbert answered in an injured tone.

Gillian interrupted. "Murray, I have things to do. Do you mind if I leave Gilbert with you? I'll stop by just before noon to see how he's doing."

Murray agreed, muttering under his breath. Then aloud answered, "Okay, but why don't you stop back around ten?"

Gillian nodded and walked away from the comical scene. She was just about to reach her cabin when Kyle called her. "What are you doing up so early on your day off?"

"You wouldn't believe me if I told you," Gillian answered as she walked back to where he was standing.

"Try me," Kyle grinned.

"Have you met Gilbert Roscoe?"

"Yes, I'm sorry to say I have."

"I promised to show him around today, so he woke me up at five-thirty and wanted me to cook his breakfast."

"And you did?" Kyle asked incredulously.

"I can't believe it either. Anyway, he wanted to go hunting, so I took him down to the riflery range and he's wreaking havoc on Murray's morning."

"Poor man," Kyle sighed.

"Gilbert?" Gillian asked.

"No, Murray," Kyle answered and laughed. "Gilbert fairly ruined Randy yesterday. Our stableman spent the rest of the day muttering obscenities to himself. It was almost funny."

"Well, I'm not laughing. What am I going to do with him for the rest of the day? Murray basically said that he wouldn't put up with him past ten o'clock."

"I'd love to help you, but we're running a busy schedule at the stables today, so I couldn't slip out. Randy certainly won't put up with him again."

"I guess I'll just have to stick it out on my own, then."

"You're a duck," Kyle said affectionately, his eyes twinkling.

"Thanks," answered Gillian halfheartedly, "but I think I'm better described as 'bird-brained.' I hope I live through this."

"If you do," Kyle said with a chuckle, "I'll see you at eight for chess. That should lift your spirits."

Gillian retorted a good-natured insult and turned to stroll back to her cabin. Her mind buzzed with ideas of what she could do with Gilbert. There really were many activities for the campers, but she couldn't think of any that were foolproof.

When she at last dragged herself back to the riflery range to rescue Murray, she found that Gilbert had already left the area.

"We had to ask him to leave," Murray explained. "He almost shot himself in the foot, then saw a pop can sitting on the fence railing and tried to shoot it off. He missed, of course, but came very close to hitting a camper's new truck sitting behind it. I can't understand how a man could really be that foolish."

"Do you know where he went?"

"He said something about going boating and I wasn't about to stop him. I know John is down there. He can figure out what to do with him. I give up."

Gillian walked away slowly and tried to think of a way to talk Gilbert into helping her in the kitchen or something else that was safe. When she arrived at the dock, Gilbert was having a canoeing lesson and seemed to be doing well. Suddenly he spied her and jumped up to wave. The canoe teetered for a few seconds and then Gilbert plunged headlong into the water.

The men nearby fished him out and brought him back to shore. Though he was drenched and shivering in the cold air, he smiled brightly and said he liked canoeing and wanted to try again tomorrow.

"Don't you think you'd better dry off now?" Gillian asked.

"Yes," he answered thoughtfully, "then I'd like to learn to use a motorboat."

"I could use your help, Gilbert," Gillian said, trying to sound sincere. "I've got some work to do in the kitchen. Would you like to stop by there after you put on some dry clothes?"

Gilbert agreed and hustled off down the path toward his cabin. Gillian sighed deeply and walked away to the kitchen. She wasn't sure how Gilbert would do, but the kitchen had to be safer than anywhere else in the camp.

She decided to do some much-needed baking and hoped Sharon wouldn't feel she was intruding. After explaining the situation to Sharon, though, she found her more than willing to help out.

When Gilbert arrived, he immediately took over. Gillian had been making a birthday cake for Carl Brooks, one of the senior staff members. They had planned to surprise him with it at supper that night. Gilbert volunteered to finish the cake and Gillian gave in to him, uncertain if she was doing the right thing.

To Gillian's surprise, Gilbert seemed to be very capable in the kitchen and she gradually relaxed. When the cake was done baking, Gilbert pulled it carefully out of the oven and set it on a rack to cool. The cake was lightly brown and perfectly shaped. Surprised, Gillian praised Gilbert over and over. He beamed at her and Gillian caught a look of childish delight in his eyes. It made her wonder if he was ever praised for his actions.

After the cake had cooled, Gillian trimmed off the rough edges while Gilbert mixed the icing. As she waited, Gillian looked down at the scraps of cake lying on the counter and she began to wonder just how good Gilbert's cake would be. When he wasn't watching, she stole a biteful and chewed it slowly. Suddenly her mouth grew tight and she rushed for a drink of water.

"Gilbert," she asked when she could speak, "how much salt did you put in that cake?"

"Oh," he answered nonchalantly, "I read the recipe wrong. When it said half a teaspoon of salt, I accidentally put in sugar, so when I came to the cup of sugar, I just corrected my error by using salt there instead."

Gillian groaned and tried not to let him see her frustration. She'd have to make another cake, but she couldn't do it while he was around and risk hurting his feelings. It was just a good thing she had tasted it. She winced as she thought about what might have happened at supper.

"I have a wonderful idea!" Gillian suddenly exclaimed. "Why don't we hunt for berries?"

Gilbert looked unimpressed. "Why, Gilbert, don't you remember that the Indians often ate berries? It would be a good experience for you." As soon as she had said it, Gillian was glad she had thought of it.

"I suppose you're right," Gilbert answered, suddenly

enthusiastic. "I should learn how to scout for berries. I may be lost in the woods someday and need to fend for myself, just like in a movie I saw."

"Right," Gillian agreed, ushering him outside quickly.

Gillian took Gilbert deep into the woods so he would feel as if they were really accomplishing something of major importance with their expedition. Gilbert whistled and began to use his city version of a western twang again, but Gillian didn't mind this time. The day was beautiful and clear, and she was walking in the forest, enjoying herself fully.

"When're we gonna find them thar berries?" Gilbert asked at last.

"We don't have to go much farther," Gillian answered. "I remember a patch Sharon and I found just up ahead."

The berry patch was just where Gillian had remembered and it was loaded with plump, juicy berries. Gilbert gave a cry of delight and began to eat the largest of the crop. For a moment Gillian was perturbed that he was not saving the berries he was picking. Then she remembered that her real purpose was to take him away from the camp. She was pleased he was at least busy doing something safe.

The warming rays of the sun cut through the chilly air and fell on Gillian's face as she gazed up toward the sky. God had truly given her the best in life when He brought her to the camp. She remembered how difficult her decision had been, and now it pained her to think she had almost chosen not to come. The wild and free world around made Gillian feel glad to be alive.

"Thar sure are a lot o' berries here," Gilbert said through a mouthful of juice.

"There certainly are," Gillian smiled back. "Even more than there were when Sharon and I found this spot."

"Do you come out here very often? Into the woods just to walk, I mean," Gilbert asked, forgetting to use his self-made accent.

"As often as I possibly can," answered Gillian.

"I wish I could stay here forever and never go back to my rotten office."

"What's wrong with your office?"

Gilbert let out a deep sigh. "Nothing. It just never changes. And I'm still in the same position I've held for the last twelve years. I just can't stand the thought of going back to that same desk and working hard to end up at the same place this time next year. I'd almost rather be worse off."

"Surely it's not all that bad. You must have friends you work with, and your family must care for you."

"I don't have a family," Gilbert answered softly. "I never married. And I don't have any friends either. People say I'm a jinx and try to stay away from me. You're the closest thing I've had to a friend in ages."

Gillian's heart ached for him. She had been trying to rid herself of Gilbert all day, and now she realized how selfish she had been.

"I'm glad you think of me as a friend," Gillian responded meaningfully. "And I don't think you're boring or a jinx."

"You don't?" Gilbert sounded amazed.

"No, I don't. Sometimes people become so convinced they can't do anything right that they spend their lives unconsciously trying to prove it."

"Is that what you think I'm doing?"

"Maybe."

"I never thought of it that way. I'm glad I met you, Gillian. I'm going to try to be different."

"You don't need to be different, Gilbert," Gillian said sincerely. "If you just be yourself and open up to people like you're doing now, they'll like you."

As Gilbert and Gillian continued to talk, she was so glad she had met him. He had taught her a very important lesson about judging other people, and about loving those who seem unlovable.

When they returned to camp, Gilbert helped Gillian make another cake, and this one turned out perfectly. At supper, Gillian bragged about Gilbert's good help, and his face shone with an emotion new to him—pride.

It was all that Gillian could do to hold back the tears when she noticed how much Gilbert glowed. Who would have believed that someone as insignificant as Gillian felt could make such a difference in a man by simply showing him that she cared?

I never could have done that before I found you. Her silent prayer reached up to heaven. *Thank you, Father, for making me different. I guess I've been doubting that you changed me at all. Today you showed me how much of your love is in my heart.*

17

*T*he next afternoon, as Gillian sat quietly working in her office, there was a light knock on the door. It opened slowly and John entered.

"I'm sorry to bother you, but I wondered if you might do us a favor. I know it's short notice, but a few of the staff were talking just now and we thought it would be fun to have a cookout for supper tonight."

"That sounds like fun!" Gillian exclaimed. "What do you want me to prepare?"

"Oh, you wouldn't have to make a thing," John answered quickly. "We've done this in past years, and a few of us men really got a kick out of thinking that we ran the show. If you'll just thaw some steaks and set out lots of potatoes, we'll do the rest."

Gillian agreed. Not only was she excited about the idea of the meal outdoors, she was also glad that she would be able to have the night off from her responsibilities.

"When do you want to plan on dinner, then?"

"We'll need to get started at four-thirty."

"Okay," Gillian smiled. "I'll set out your food and then find somewhere else to go. I don't suppose you'll want me hovering over you tonight."

John smiled. "Thanks," he said and stepped out the door.

Gillian leaned back in her chair. A meal outdoors did sound like a good idea. This cool fall day was perfect for it.

She remembered many times when her father had donned his chef's hat and attempted to cook a meal on their backyard grill. Most of the time the food had been quite good, but at other times—well, at least the dog had enjoyed a special meal on those nights.

Steak and potatoes seemed like a very limited menu, though. There really should be another vegetable, and maybe a salad, too. Gillian couldn't resist the urge to add a little extra to the meal and soon found herself in the kitchen setting out ears of corn along with salad and buns.

When she at last stepped back and surveyed her work, it was obvious she had gone past the help John had requested. She wasn't sure how serious the men were about doing everything themselves, so she decided she'd better be gone before they arrived to begin the major preparations.

Gillian scooped up her jacket and slipped out the side door. She tried to sneak down the path without making it obvious, waving casually at John as she passed him, and soon was reclining comfortably on a soft grassy bank by the lake.

The afternoon sun shone brilliantly in the cloudless sky. As she relaxed, gentle waves of thought drifted on her mind. Soon she was thinking of her father again. She pictured him standing by the smoking grill with a long fork in one hand and a glass of Coke in the other. He would poke at the meat and then take a long sip from his glass. Then he would return to poking at the meat. It was not surprising that his steaks were in poor shape by the time they were set on the table. The smoke would draw her mother from the house and she would wink and make faces at Gillian when the self-appointed cook had his back turned. Then the two of them would giggle like schoolgirls.

For a long time, Gillian was lost in her dreams. A sigh escaped her and floated across the lake. It was pleasant here, but on that day the joy Gillian felt was bittersweet. Her reflections had made her heart ache for her family.

Just then Gillian noticed a deep savory odor in the air. It lured her from her daydreams, pulling her toward the camp. She jumped up and hurried down the path where she found the men laughing and joking about their work.

"Hey, Gillian," Randy called, "don't that smell better than any steak you've ever had?"

"Every year we get better at this, guys," John agreed heartily.

The men continued to bolster their egos, and other people gathered around the grill, anxious to see if the food was as good as the boastful men claimed.

"All right," Jake called out, "the first seven steaks are ready to go."

Ten men hurried to grab a plate, and a line formed beside the grill. The serving went slowly as Jake placed steak after steak on the outstretched plates before him. The men ate ravenously and Gillian began to doubt that there would be enough to feed those who were coming later.

"Here's a special steak for the special lady who allowed us to have our fun without spoiling it," Jake said as he held out a full plate and winked at her playfully.

Gillian took the food and went to sit down on a nearby stump. Cautiously she eyed the meal in front of her. She wasn't sure what she expected, but when she savored the first bite, she was surprised. It was the best steak she had ever tasted, but how it got that way remained a mystery to her.

Slowly the line at the grill shortened and people quieted while they ate the feast before them. At last, the self-acclaimed cooks set down their tools and helped themselves, patting each other on the back in great satisfaction.

Sharon came to sit beside Gillian. They couldn't help laughing as they watched the men. "This is the third year they've done this," Sharon explained, "and every year they get more obnoxious and boastful about it. They seem to think they have some special talent for cooking steaks outdoors. Everyone knows that it's the atmosphere that makes this taste so good, not the food. If we all got up right now and moved into the dining hall to eat, we'd know how bad this really is.

Gillian laughed at Sharon's theory and relished another bite of her steak. *Whatever the reason*, she thought to herself, *it really does taste good.*

After the meal was finished, Jake, Kyle, and John appeared, each carrying a guitar, and the group of men began to sing a strange, rollicking song about a crazy hunter. Gillian had never heard it before, but as the others joined in heartily, she sat and laughed at the words. Just as soon as the last notes of the song died down, a man at the back started to sing another and everyone quickly picked up the new melody. The group sang song after song, with the guitars strumming along.

Gradually the robust songs died out and were replaced by more relaxing music that floated through the evening air. The sun set slowly, blending the colors of the sky with the flames of the fire.

When the others had quieted down, Kyle began a strange song, quietly at first, then building in volume. His voice rose and fell with the mood of the song, and Gillian found herself swaying to the lilting tune.

He has a nice voice, she thought. *I wonder why he seems so distant lately. He never really talks to me like he used to.* Gillian's brow furrowed as she sat gazing into the fire, searching for the answers.

As the last chord faded, the campers dispersed, and the cooks, satisfied with the successful evening, began their cleanup.

Just as Gillian rose to help, John called out, "Jake, I think this young lady is going to try to help us. Why don't you walk her back to her cabin and see that she doesn't get in the way here?"

Jake smiled and turned to offer Gillian his arm. They walked together in the coolness of the night, where the spell of the songs still lingered in the rustle of the trees, and the laughter of the other men slowly faded behind them.

"You seem very pensive tonight," Jake commented.

"Does it show that much?"

"Oh, I don't think anyone else noticed, but you're just not looking around as you walk. You usually do, you know."

"Well," Gillian blushed, uncertain whether to divulge her feelings to Jake, "I have been a little confused lately."

"About Kyle, right?" Jake added perceptively.

"How did you know?"

"You've both been acting strangely. Did you have a fight?"

"No," Gillian quickly answered, and then stopped. "At least, I don't think so. Maybe I did say something to upset him, but I can't imagine what it could be. It seems like ever since I started helping out at the stables, just when I thought we were getting pretty close, he hasn't wanted to be near me or really talk to me."

Jake paused for a moment and then stated openly, "He watches you, you know."

"What do you mean?" Gillian asked.

"Sometimes I see him looking in your direction with a confused look on his face. I've never known Kyle to be so thoughtful all the time."

Frustration returned to Gillian. "Well, I can't imagine what he spends so much time thinking about. Everything was so simple for a while and now nothing makes sense. I can't talk to him and he doesn't seem to want to talk to me. There's nothing I can think of to change all that."

Jake smiled deep inside himself and then answered, "Remember Sarah? She kept me guessing for so long, but it all worked out in the end. If I were you, I would just hold on for a little while longer. It might be that Kyle needs time to sort something out in his mind. Don't give up on him, though. If my guess is right, he's not even close to writing you off. Just be patient—and extra friendly—and you can't lose. After all," he added playfully, "who could resist those pretty green eyes?"

18

*F*all weekends were a busy time of the year. Businessmen from all fields were eager to escape the busy events of the week and spend some time unwinding. The staff found it difficult to keep up with the men, the few groups of students on weekend class trips, and nature buffs who all seemed to want to arrive on Friday and leave late Sunday.

All the activity made the days fly past, though. Gillian spent most of her extra time sitting alone with her Bible, trying to catch up on what she had missed by never attending Sunday school. She imagined that those around her were getting tired of her many questions, so she tried to do what she could to discover God's truths on her own.

A problem soon began to arise, however. Gillian found that the more she began to know about the Bible, the more she realized how little she knew. It was a never-ending circle—but a challenging one. She also found that what she read in the morning often had a very direct application for the day. It was exciting how easily she could use her new-found wisdom to meet the needs of her life.

————

Fall breezes were soon pushed away by winter winds sweeping down from the glaciers, carrying with them the chill of the ice itself. Jack Frost worked his magic in the stillness of the morning, painting the windows and freezing the tender plants. It was clear winter was on its way.

One morning, after sleeping fitfully during the night, Gillian woke suddenly. Feeling the bitter cold of the room around her, she pulled the quilt up to her ears. She could not remember it being so cold in her cabin before.

When at last she struggled out from the security of her bed, she realized why she had slept so poorly. During the night, a winter storm had crept through the camp, covering the world with a heavy blanket of glistening snow.

Gillian struggled with a fire in the wood stove that she had neglected for so long, then walked timidly to the window. A thick layer of ice made it difficult to see outside, but she rubbed at it until it melted.

The clearing in front of her cabin was completely white, blinding her eyes momentarily with its brilliance. When she could see clearly again, she noticed that the snow covered everything around her. Only the trees stood above it, and they were weighted down by the heavy clumps of snow hanging stubbornly to their branches.

As she stood at the window, she saw a strange lumbering figure struggling along what used to be the path to her cabin. Gillian soon realized with relief that it was a person.

"Gillian," a man's voice called.

Gillian flew to the door and pushed against it, but it wouldn't budge. She pushed again and it moved only slightly.

"Gillian," he called again.

"I'm here!" she yelled back from the window. "I can't get out."

"I know," he answered, closer this time. "The snow is piled against the screen door. We'll have to shovel you out." Gillian had a sudden feeling of panic. The thought of being held prisoner in her cabin by the snow was frightening.

"How long will it take?" she asked, trying to speak calmly.

The man was now at the window. She could see him

standing on snow only a couple of feet lower than the glass itself. It was Jake.

"It won't be long," he answered reassuringly. "I've already dug out several of the others, and they'll be here shortly with shovels to help me with the rest of the cabins."

Gillian was comforted more by Jake's presence than his words, and she sunk back into a chair to wait for her rescuers.

It did not take long before the other men arrived and Gillian could hear the sound of shovels grating against the snow. The steady rhythm stirred her to life and she hurriedly dressed in the chilly bedroom.

When the door was finally opened, Gillian sighed with relief. Jake emerged carrying a heavy parka and huge boots, which he set behind the door.

"We've closed the camp down for today because of the snow that has already fallen. And more is supposed to be on the way. The men with me are going to deliver food to each of the cabins later, so you don't need to report to the kitchen. You should stay put if you can," Jake warned, "but if you need to go out, wear this parka. It's also important for you to stay on the paths. The place looks very different with all this snow and it's easy to get lost. If you do, there's not much chance that someone will be able to find you, so you've got to be very careful." Jake stopped for a moment and then added, "We've got to dig some more people out. Will you be okay here?"

Gillian assured Jake and he left, closing the door firmly behind him. The feeling of helplessness returned to her and she paced back and forth, wondering what to do.

Soon Gillian felt as if she couldn't stand it any longer. She pulled the parka awkwardly around her and then struggled with the boots. Looking in the mirror, she saw a strange Eskimo staring back at her. She laughed at her unfamiliar image.

Slowly she walked to the door, almost afraid to open it to the strange world. The snow twinkled like a thousand tiny stars that had fallen during the night. Gillian stepped solemnly onto the cleared patch in front of her cabin and closed the door behind her.

Carefully, she made her way across the pile of snow that had drifted around her cabin in the night. It was difficult to move because her boots sunk deeply into the snow with every step, but eventually she arrived at where she thought the path would have been.

Having no definite plan for her hike, she started toward the lake to see if it had frozen over yet. After walking several yards and still not seeing the lake, Gillian decided not to take the chance of misjudging the distance to the water's edge and falling in.

The path leading to the camp was quite worn because of the many boots which had already traveled over it, so Gillian set out in that direction. It was difficult going and she was soon exhausted from the effort of pushing one foot ahead of the other in the deep snow.

"That's not the best way to move through snow," Kyle's voice called through the trees.

Gillian looked around her as best she could and still could not spot him anywhere. "Where are you?" she called.

"I'm standing on my porch," he answered.

Gillian peered through the trees in the direction of Kyle's cabin and then she could see it. She made her way toward him and eventually emerged in front of the cabin.

"How did you know I was there?" Gillian asked inquisitively.

"I heard someone muttering and I wanted to know who it was," Kyle answered with a grin, while producing a pair of binoculars from behind his back, "so I had to take a look."

"I'll bet I looked silly," Gillian smiled, with a slow blush rising in her cheeks.

"Why don't you come in and warm yourself?" Kyle changed the subject. "Then I'll show you how the professionals get around outdoors in the winter."

Gillian could not turn down the offer of a warm place to rest, so she kicked the snow from her pantlegs as best she could and walked into the little cabin.

The fire was burning cheerfully, with a steaming pot of hot water sitting toward the back of the stove. Kyle made two cups of hot chocolate while Gillian pulled off her boots and parka. It was so good to be free of their burdensome weight.

"What brings you out on such a nasty day?" Kyle asked as he set the cups on the table in front of them.

"I just couldn't stand to be cooped up," Gillian responded. "It was all right until I knew that I couldn't leave. Then I had to get out as soon as I had the chance."

"I know what you mean. The first winter I spent here we were snowed in for three days and the snow just wouldn't stop falling. A few people climbed out of windows, but we were all advised to stay put. I thought I'd go crazy."

Gillian giggled at the thought of Kyle pacing about his cabin.

"Do you believe I actually took up knitting to pass the time? Kate had asked me to pick up some supplies for her while I was in town the day before and I hadn't had a chance to deliver them. I shelved my pride and taught myself in a day. I made a sock. Would you like to see it?"

"I'd love to!" exclaimed Gillian, and Kyle set off to find his prize. He returned with the sorriest-looking bundle of knots that Gillian had ever seen, but she smiled mercifully and just said, "It's nice."

Kyle looked at it almost lovingly and set it down on the shelf. "It kept me occupied for an entire day anyway," he sighed. "But I wore out the instruction book, I had to refer to it so often."

"Does this happen all winter long—being snowed in, I mean?" Gillian was quite concerned.

"No, no. Once the screen doors have been taken off there's no problem, but the first snow sometimes catches us off guard."

Gillian was very relieved. They sat in silence for a while, sipping contendedly at their hot chocolate. When it was gone, Gillian felt much better.

"Would you like to play a game?" Kyle asked.

"Sure. What do you have—besides chess?"

"Only a deck of Rook cards. Do you know how to play Rook?" Kyle asked, expecting to hear she didn't.

"Yes," Gillian answered. "It's the only game my family plays at reunions."

Gillian poured them each another cup of hot chocolate while Kyle dealt the cards. It was not long until the two were engrossed in the game and time seemed to fly. Kyle found that Gillian was a very good player and was soon far ahead of him in points. Gillian could not help but take every opportunity to repeat the score to him. Kyle, however, didn't seem to mind. In fact, he seemed to enjoy it.

Suddenly a knock at the door interrupted their game. Kyle rose quickly and opened it to find Randy holding a large bag.

Seeing Gillian sitting there, he shifted the bag awkwardly and looked meaningfully at Kyle, as if asking a silent question. "This is your food in case we get more snow and we're stuck for a couple days," he said, explaining his appearance.

"Would you like to come in and join us for a while?" Kyle asked jovially, ignoring the look.

"No," Randy answered quickly. "I've got quite a few more supplies to deliver," and he was gone.

"He acted very strange," Gillian commented.

"He's probably just cold and tired," Kyle stated in an effort to evade the issue.

Kyle put the food away and set a large bag of potato chips in front of them while they resumed the game. It didn't take Gillian much longer to beat him, and they sat back in their chairs to chat for a while.

"I'd better be going," Gillian said after some time. "It's almost lunch and all I had for breakfast was potato chips."

"You're welcome to eat here," Kyle quickly responded.

"No, I don't want to impose," Gillian answered, "and besides, I should be getting back. They probably left my supplies outside my door and I'll have to thaw out my lunch before I can eat it."

They both laughed at the thought, and Gillian climbed back into the heavy coat and monstrous boots.

"I don't think I'll ever get used to these things. I don't see how the Eskimos move fast enough to catch their dinner," Gillian muttered, half joking.

"Ah, but there never was a prettier little Eskimo," Kyle winked and held the door for her while she struggled back out into the glistening snow.

Had Gillian imagined the remark? No, Kyle had really said it. Maybe Jake was right. Maybe Kyle had just needed time. She replayed the compliment over in her mind as she crunched through the snow.

Gillian spent the rest of the day writing letters and munching on snacks. It became dark even earlier than usual that evening because of another storm making its way over the horizon, and Gillian found it useless to try to keep herself awake.

She read her Bible before she snuggled down and fell asleep dreaming of Jesus talking with Martha and Mary—and herself.

19

The next day, Gillian rose very late. She wasn't sure if her sudden unquenchable need for sleep was somewhat like a bear feels in hibernation or if she had just become lazy. She fixed a light brunch and read a book by the stove where she could feel toasty warm.

Early in the afternoon, she heard a knock on the door and hurriedly went to answer it, glad for the interruption. Kyle stood outside with a wide grin on his face. He wore a strange outfit with gray corduroy knickers, a heavy sweater, a red ski hat, and brightly colored socks.

"I promised to show you how to travel in the snow efficiently yesterday and I never did. How would you like your first lesson?"

Gillian scrambled into her parka and joined Kyle outside. She noticed that he was standing on skis with another pair leaned against the wall.

"You expect me to allow you to make me look that silly?" she scoffed.

"No one will notice the difference," Kyle answered. His blue eyes twinkled and his mustache twitched when he added, "Besides, it's very easy to learn to cross-country ski, and I'm sure that even you could do it."

Gillian laughed at his playful insult. "Don't you dare underestimate me," she teased back. "I happen to learn new skills very quickly."

Kyle laughed and handed her a pair of cross-country

ski shoes. After Gillian had put on the oversized shoes and tucked her pantlegs into her socks, Kyle helped her secure the flat black extension at the toe of her shoe into the fitting on the skis. Before long he was gliding across the open space beside the path, with Gillian struggling to keep up.

Kyle was a good teacher and Gillian was soon moving smoothly across the snow, although not very quickly, and the two set out down the path toward the center of camp.

The day was crisp and clear, and Gillian found that she enjoyed skiing very much. It was much easier to move now that she no longer sunk knee-deep into the snow with every step.

They skied past the center of the camp and started down the trail to the stables where Kyle wanted to check on his colt. Gillian could hear the distant voice of the wind stirring the trees on the mountain above her, but it no longer blew angrily as it had the day before it brought the storm.

The colt was secured and the other horses fed and watered. Kyle led the way back down the path they had already traveled, and they skied toward the hub of the camp.

Gillian breathed deeply in pleasure. Then suddenly her senses snapped to alertness. There was a faint, almost imperceptible smell of smoke, but it seemed to be getting rapidly stronger. She scanned the forest around her to try to detect where it had come from, but she could see nothing.

She noticed that Kyle was also looking around him, sniffing the air.

"Do you smell anything?" he called back to her.

"Yes," she answered. "Do you think it's only the smoke from all the stoves?"

"It could be, but it doesn't smell like burning wood."

Gillian could sense that Kyle wanted to hurry to investigate the possible danger, but was holding himself in check for her sake.

"If you want to go ahead, I'll be all right," she called.

"Are you sure?"

"Of course," Gillian answered. "All I have to do is follow the tracks we made in the snow on the way here."

Kyle looked over his shoulder and nodded to her, then sped off down the path to find the source of the smoke.

Gillian watched him glide away from her and around the bend. She felt alone and frightened at first, but then realized that God was with her and that His presence should be even more comforting than Kyle's had been. She started to talk to Him about her fears, allowing His peace to pervade her spirit.

When she arrived at the center of camp, she saw that it was bustling with activity. Men were doing their best to scurry around in the deep snow, carrying buckets and other containers.

"Is it a fire?" Gillian asked a man as he rushed past her.

"Yes," he called over his shoulder. "One of the campers stocked his stove too high and some of the sparks that flew up the stovepipe caught fire on the roof. The water pipes near those cabins are frozen, so we have to carry the water from here."

Gillian hurried to the kitchen with the thought of finding more containers for water. Just as she approached the door, a man stumbled around the corner, struggling to carry two heavy buckets of water in the deep snow.

"Hey, can I borrow your skis?" he asked, sweat draining off his face.

"Of course," Gillian answered and hurried to step out of them. The man forced the toes of his own shoes into the clasps of the skis and continued on much more quickly and easily, leaving the poles behind.

Gillian walked into the kitchen and looked carefully around. The shelves had been stripped of any container that was large enough to carry water to the fire. Gillian could think of nothing more to do, so she sat in her office and tried to work on some much-neglected plans. The minutes ticked by slowly and Gillian soon found herself pacing restlessly in front of the windows.

Men scurried back and forth while the smoke grew thick above the trees. With no one to keep her updated, Gillian's mind pictured a desperate scene. She was worried that the fire would spread to neighboring cabins and into the trees. Kyle had said it was difficult to stop a large fire once it began.

"Dear God," she prayed fervently, "please don't let the fire spread. Please protect the camp!"

After what seemed like hours, men began to filter back toward the center of camp, mopping their foreheads and rubbing soot from their faces with dirty hands.

When Gillian saw their tired, limp bodies, she snapped into action. Surely they would be thirsty. She called to them to come into the dining hall for something to drink and quickly started to prepare juice and cake.

The men nearest the dining hall filed in and slumped into the chairs. Others followed and a line of tired firefighters moved slowly through the doors.

The men were quieter than Gillian had ever seen them. None of them seemed to be in the mood to talk. They simply drank their juice and leaned heavily on the table. The cake remained untouched on its tray.

Not able to stand the tension any longer, Gillian asked one of the men as he was helping himself to more juice, "How bad was it?"

"We lost them," he muttered, unable to meet her gaze.

"Lost them—lost who?" Gillian asked urgently, but the man had already returned to his seat.

Panic gripped her and she scanned the crowd carefully. Her thoughts flew to Kyle. He hadn't returned yet. It couldn't be!

Desperately, she ran out the kitchen door, taking time only to grab her coat before rushing down the trail the men had beaten into the snow.

When she reached the cabin, she stopped in her tracks. The building was no more than an empty shell of black charred boards. The snow around it was covered with soot, and the stench of the smoke still hung heavily in the air. Gillian summoned enough courage to move closer and noticed that the men standing in front of the cabin were gathered around a covered body lying on the snow.

Solemnly and fearfully she approached the men. Her gaze refused to fall to the body below her. Instead, she intently searched the faces of the men standing around it. Kyle was not there.

Tears began to stream down her cheeks and she felt her stomach knot. She heard one of the men standing close to her say they were bringing the other victim out. Gillian couldn't stand it and turned away from the horrible scene.

From far down the path she saw another man running with a black bag swinging in one of his hands. Gillian supposed he must be a doctor that had been called earlier and was just arriving, too late to be of any help.

"Doctor Hayes," John called out thankfully. When the doctor had arrived beside him, gasping for breath, he continued, "There are two men who didn't make it and another three hurt. One of them pretty bad. The whole thing caved in when two of the workers from the camp went in to save the man inside. They didn't know it was already too late. One of them is lying over there and the other is inside the cabin across from us." The doctor cast a glance toward the fatally injured men and then hurried across the yard to the men who had been hurt.

Gillian could picture Kyle rushing in to save the life of a man already lost, and her tears started again. But the man had said there were two staff members who went in. The other would-be rescuer was in the cabin across from her, and Gillian quickly moved toward it. She told herself vaguely that she wanted to see if there was anything she could do for him, but mostly she felt a need to escape from the scene of the fire's terrible destruction.

When she entered the building, it took a moment for her eyes to adjust to the darkness inside. Before she could focus clearly, she heard a quick movement and felt strong arms encircle her.

Gillian jerked her head up and gasped when she realized it was Kyle. Relief flooded over her and she laid her head on his chest and sobbed openly.

When at last she gained control of herself, she looked up slowly and whispered, "I thought you were the one—" but she couldn't find the right words to finish her sentence.

Kyle looked at her bravely through red, puffy eyes and said quietly, "You thought it was me who was killed?"

Gillian nodded.

"Gillian," he continued after seating her on a nearby chair and taking a deep breath, "I was hurt in the fire, but I'll be okay. But the other—" A tear squeezed out of his eye and ran down his cheek. It was a moment before he could continue. "Another man was killed. Did you know that?"

"Yes," she answered, uncomprehending.

"Do you know who the other man was?" At Gillian's response, he continued slowly, "It was Jake."

Agony swept through her and she felt her last bit of strength drain away. She was hardly aware of Kyle's arms supporting her while she wept uncontrollably. She could hear him speaking to her sporadically in low tones and crying softly.

"We both went in to find the man. When we got there, we realized it was too late for him. But before we had a chance to get out, the roof caved in. Jake pushed me forward and told me to run. I did—just as fast as I could. I thought he was right behind me. When the roof caved in, Jake was trapped by one of the beams. I tried to get back in, but there was just no way. I was outside and there wasn't even a cabin left for me to run into. It was completely gone. There was no way I could get to him, and I knew he couldn't have made it even before they brought his body out."

For a long time they cried together and then Kyle pulled himself up stiffly. "The doctor wants to bandage my hands. I'd better let him do that now."

Gillian nodded and sat back in her chair. As Kyle turned to the doctor, a numbed feeling rose inside Gillian and she stared blankly into space. She had no more strength to cope with the tragedy, and her emotions tightened inside her to retreat from the pain.

Time dragged by and finally the doctor released Kyle, telling him to be sure to get plenty of rest in the next few days. Kyle helped Gillian to her feet and they moved out the door.

For the first time, Gillian noted how badly Kyle had been burned. His brightly colored socks were shredded and black, and his sweater was badly torn. His face was smeared with soot and ashes, and his hair was plastered to his head with sweat.

"I don't know where the pair of skis went that you lent me," Gillian apologized, suddenly feeling that this was important. "I lent them to a man I didn't know so he could move more quickly when he brought the water."

"That's okay," Kyle answered. "I don't remember what I did with mine either."

The day that had started out so well had ended in chaos and tragedy. As the two walked slowly down the path supporting each other, Gillian found herself wishing she had not accepted Kyle's offer to ski. In some strange twist of her thinking, it seemed that if she had done something—anything else—the whole day might have turned out differently.

Gillian walked Kyle to his cabin and helped him remove what was left of his shoes and socks. He refused to eat, but Gillian persuaded him to drink a glass of water before he collapsed onto his bed in exhaustion. After wiping his face with a cool, damp cloth, Gillian left him and returned to her own cabin. With no thought of feeding herself, she stumbled into her bedroom and threw herself down on the bed. As she struggled to find a comfortable position, her eyes fell on the Bible lying on the table beside the bed. The book reminded her of Jake and seemed to force her to face the tragedy, making her tears flow again.

"Why Jake?" Gillian cried aloud. "He was such a good man. Why couldn't it have been someone else? And why did it have to be anyone at all? Couldn't someone do something to stop it?" Suddenly Gillian choked miserably as a horrible thought entered her mind. "You could have stopped it," she whispered breathlessly. "Why didn't you, God? Why did you let Jake die? He was the man who did the most to help me find you. How could you do this to him? Is that how you reward a man who loves you and spends his life serving you?"

When Gillian realized the full meaning of what she was saying, she burst into sobs. "I'm sorry," she cried. "I didn't mean to say those things. I just don't understand. Why should a man like Jake have to be the one to die when there are so many others who don't seem to have a reason to live at all? I loved Jake, Lord. He was one of the best friends I ever had and certainly about the best person I ever knew."

For a moment Gillian groped for words. "I'm going to miss him so much," she said faintly. "I know he's with you and he's happier, but I miss him already. Please take care of him for me. And help me to try to live like he showed me to." A tear trickled down her cheek as she finished softly, "I wish I would have told him that I loved him."

For a long time, Gillian lay on her bed crying. The bitterness had been taken away, but the sorrow was still a heavy weight. She longed for her father's strong embrace more now than ever since she had come to the camp. Hours passed before she fell into the comfort of sleep.

20

The next few days were difficult. Kyle was in poor spirits because he had been told to rest in his cabin, and this gave him no opportunity to escape his grief. Gillian often visited and tried to cheer him up, but her successes were short-lived. Kyle grew more and more impatient to help the other staff members dig the camp out of the snow, but his blistered hands made it impossible.

A short funeral service for Jake was to be held shortly after the noon meal at the camp the day before his body would be transferred to his family. The entire camp was quiet and melancholy on that day. People moved slowly, almost reverently, through every activity in making the final preparations.

Gillian found that she also had a difficult time functioning normally. Everything seemed to remind her of Jake, and she would have to shut her eyes tightly to keep the tears from coming.

Gillian hurried through preparation of the noon meal in order to have time to change her clothes and wash up.

She wished now that she had brought just one dress with her, but she never dreamed she would need one this far out in the wilderness. Just as she was putting the final touches on her hair, she heard a light knock on the door and ran to open it.

"Are you ready?" Kyle asked quietly. Gillian felt sorry for Kyle. He had not been the same since the fire, and his eyes held the pain of hours spent alone in the torment of an awful memory.

"Almost," Gillian answered. "Come in."

Kyle walked slowly into the room and stood looking out the window while Gillian pulled on her coat and boots.

"It seems disrespectful to wear pants to a funeral," she remarked, as if to herself.

When she looked up at Kyle, she saw a slow tear run down his cheek. Immediately she was sorry she had spoken so thoughtlessly.

"Kyle," she spoke softly, laying a hand on his shoulder, "I didn't mean to make you feel worse. I'm sorry."

"It wasn't what you said, really," Kyle whispered hoarsely. "I've just been thinking how Jake deserves much better than this." As soon as he had voiced the thought, Kyle lost control of his emotions and lowered his head to hide his tears.

After a moment Gillian turned to pick up Jake's Bible and whispered, "We'd better go." Kyle followed and they fell in with the streams of people who were making their way to the lodge for the service.

It was difficult for Kyle and Gillian to find a seat in the crowded room. Its purpose was for smaller gatherings, so many people were already standing at the back. At last they slid onto a bench that was built around the firepit.

Gillian had attended only one funeral before in her life, when she was much younger. The whole atmosphere seemed foreign to her. She hoped it would always feel that way. She never wanted to feel comfortable at a funeral.

The casket lay closed at the front of the building. There were a few scattered houseplants that Gillian knew must be Kate's, but besides them, the only decorations were some candles and a satin cloth draped over the box.

Gillian tried to imagine Jake's body lying in the casket, but she found it was impossible. To picture Jake as a man beaten by any natural force seemed like a contradiction. Jake had always been a man that Gillian looked to whenever she had questions or problems. He always seemed to have the right answer.

There had been times when he had sensed her question even before she had been brave enough to ask it. His patience with her surpassed anyone else's that she knew.

John rose reverently to signal the beginning of the service, and the crowd hushed. He moved to a microphone set at the front and paused for a moment in silence.

"I'm not much of a public speaker," he said at last. "That's always been Jake's department." There was another pause as if he were fighting for control. "Since I don't consider myself worthy to give any kind of sermon today, I thought I would just tell you what Jake means to me and then let anyone else speak who wants to.

"I met Jake six years ago when he spoke at a youth rally in my hometown. He wasn't one of the most dynamic speakers that I had heard, but he had a quality that really impressed me. It was his honesty.

"There had been many teachers in my life. Many men who tried to show me what it was to live a Christ-centered life, but few of them had any effect on me. I just didn't see much in them that I wanted for myself. They were good men, but I thought they were too good, almost to the point of being untouchable.

"Jake showed me that a person doesn't have to be Superman to be a Christian—that God only requires two things of those who serve Him. He wants us to honestly and sincerely work to serve Him, but, more importantly, to give *Him* all of our struggles, failures, and faults. It's only when we live in His strength instead of our own that we can have victory in our lives. I never knew that before.

"When I started this camp some years later, I knew that Christ should be the center of everything in my life, so I naturally wanted to bring that out in my camp. I made inquiries about Jake and found that he was living in a small town in Alberta. His wife had recently died and he had decided to stop touring and settle down in order to be close to his family.

"I thought he wouldn't be interested, but when I approached him about the camp anyway, he seemed to jump at the offer. He told me that he had been feeling very uncomfortable because he knew God wanted him to continue preaching, but He didn't seem to be leading him in any definite direction. So Jake came to the camp that following summer. He made friends quickly with the staff and has been teaching us about the Bible ever since.

"When I was a teenager, it often bothered me when Paul wrote that we should strive to be like him. I couldn't see how any man could be so righteous that he would dare tell others to follow his example when they were struggling with the idea of being like Christ. Jake never said that about himself—but he certainly could have.

"I've never known a man—" John's head turned away for a moment and he paused. When he faced the audience again, there was a large tear trickling down his cheek. "I've never known a man I wanted to imitate more than I do Jake."

Gillian heard the sound of people all around her agreeing with John and also the sound of sniffles.

"I'm finished," John said awkwardly, after a moment. "Is there anyone else who would like to say something?"

People began to shuffle uncomfortably and then quieted again as Terry Holt, the young woman who worked as a receptionist and bookkeeper for the camp, stepped forward. She had tears running down her face and a tissue firmly gripped in one hand, but she walked up to the microphone, determined to speak her mind.

After she cleared her throat twice, she began. "Jake was like a father to me. I came to this camp a confused little girl, and he made me feel like I belonged here right away. Somehow he knew that I wasn't the strong person I pretended to be. I'm not sure how he knew. He was the first person to see it.

"Many times he talked to me about God, and many times I didn't listen. I know it hurt him but I just couldn't understand." Terry sniffed and continued. "I asked him so many times how someone could love a stranger enough to die for him. I just couldn't believe it was true." There was another long pause and then the girl burst out, "Jake did. He loved people so much that he didn't even think about himself when he tried to save the man he didn't know."

A stifled sob caught in Gillian's throat, and she saw Kyle lower his head.

"I know he can't hear me, but I just want to say that I believe now, Jake. And I hope that God will tell you that I've finally given in. Thanks for trying so hard. If it hadn't been for you, I never would have learned what I have these last two days."

Terry stepped down and Kate went quickly to hug her. Everyone sat watching as she turned from Kate and walked to the casket. Her fingers traveled slowly over the decorative trim, and then she turned quickly and returned to her seat.

There was a long silence and everyone was beginning to feel uncomfortable. Then a stout little woman walked forward from the back of the room and took her place at the microphone. Gillian at once recognized Aunt Lucy.

"There is just too much sadness in this room," she announced firmly. "I am Jake's aunt and I know him well enough to know that, even though he might be flattered for a moment, Jake would not want us to go on crying and grieving like this."

There were several shocked people whose sharp intakes of breath said they thought it very appropriate to grieve at a funeral, but their gasps didn't bother Aunt Lucy.

"Jake would have been the first one to admit that he isn't lying in that casket down there. Oh, his body is, but that's not what you're saying you'll miss. The real Jake is up in heaven, singing and shouting and praising the God he's worked to please all his life. I don't suppose there's any other place he would rather be.

"I loved my nephew. And I know that he loved me, too, but I also know that he was a man of God. Death held no fear or remorse for him. Let's not dampen that sense of victory here. Let's just spend a moment picturing Jake before the throne of God and send up a cheer. That's what Jake would want the most."

Aunt Lucy stepped down from the microphone and walked directly to the casket. With all eyes on her she turned her gaze sharply up to heaven and shouted, "Praise the Lord, for Jake is with his Maker today. May we all grow as close to our God as he did."

People stirred at the sudden outburst and there were several who uttered "Amen" and "Praise the Lord" in return. Aunt Lucy turned and placed a hand on the casket. After a moment she nodded her head and walked back to her seat.

John waited only a moment before he moved to the microphone and dismissed the service.

The shuffling of feet filled the air and Gillian stood slowly. She felt Kyle rise beside her and looked over to him. His face shone as he looked down at her and said simply, "I was wrong. This funeral service was good enough for Jake. He would have been truly pleased."

Randy was relieved that the service was over. He was experiencing so many conflicting emotions that he just wanted to get away. He did love and respect Jake, but he still couldn't accept what Jake believed about God. *It was easy for Jake—it's easy for all of these people,* he reasoned inwardly.

They haven't faced what I have in life. If there's a God, why did He let my mother die? No, a God who takes my mom and the only man I look up to is no God at all. Randy couldn't run out the door fast enough.

21

*T*he winter settled in and Gillian grew adjusted to its moods. Many days she rose to find snow blowing across the grounds, while the next day would be clear with a cheerful sun smiling on the camp. Often she thought of Jake and all he had told her about nature and having respect for it. At times she grew very lonely for him. Kyle resumed his work cautiously, but his hands remained very tender for quite some time.

One afternoon Kyle burst through the kitchen door just as Gillian was finishing menus for the next week.

Gillian could tell from the look on his face that he had something to tell her.

"All right, Kyle," Gillian gave in, "what exciting news do you have?"

"Guess," Kyle answered with a boyish grin.

"I won the lottery," Gillian teased back. "No, that can't be it because I didn't buy a ticket."

"Guess again," Kyle prodded.

"Just tell me," she returned impatiently.

"We're planning a trip."

"Who's 'we,' and where are 'we' going?"

"We is the staff and we're going skiing."

"That's not a trip, Kyle," Gillian muttered back. "And we've gone skiing a lot lately."

"That's not what I mean," Kyle grinned again. "We're going downhill skiing at the Lake Louise ski resort."

"I can't downhill ski," winced Gillian.

"You'll learn. You learned to cross-country ski very quickly."

"But when I fell down then, I just fell down. If I fall on the side of a mountain, I'll roll all the way down to the bottom. That doesn't sound like much fun."

"You won't roll down the mountain," Kyle answered mockingly. "You'd smash into a tree first."

Kyle laughed at his own joke, but Gillian walked away with a toss of her head and pretended to be busy.

"Be a sport, Gillian," Kyle said, following her across the room. "I promise to teach you. I'll stay with you on the bunny hills all day if I have to."

"What are bunny hills?" Gillian inquired.

"They're the beginner slopes," he answered hastily, knowing he was winning. "They're short and not too steep so that beginners, like yourself, won't get hurt."

"Will you promise not to leave me there alone?" Gillian asked slowly.

"I solemnly promise," Kyle said, looking deeply into her eyes.

Gillian noticed his mustache twitching playfully and stepped away. "I'll go, but I don't think I'll like it."

———

Two days later Gillian found herself in an overloaded van rolling down the highway toward the ski slopes. She still had misgivings about trying a sport that was so dangerous, but Kyle had not let her back out.

"We're almost there," someone called from the front of the van. "We'll rent our skis here at Lake Louise Village and then hurry out to the slopes before there is much of a crowd."

The group had set out very early that morning, wanting to rent skis while there was still a large supply. By the time they all came out of the rental office, it was still only nine o'clock, yet some of the more avid skiers were getting impatient to go. Gillian could have waited much longer, but she hurried for the sake of the others.

Since there would be no place to leave their own footwear outside the lodge, the group had to put their ski boots on before leaving the area and walk the remainder of the distance in them. Gillian was surprised at how difficult it was. The shaft of the boots sloped quite far forward at the ankles so that the skier could maintain a good position for moving downhill, but it made the boots very cumbersome to walk in. She unbuckled them as best she could to make movement easier, but they were still heavy and awkward.

There was not much of a line waiting to buy tickets since it was a weekday, so they moved quickly to the other side of the lodge where they would put on their skis and be swept away by the tow lifts.

Gillian stood gazing at the long slopes stretching in front of her and almost held her breath. They looked so steep. Small swarms of skiers were already traveling over the slopes, looking like tiny ants on the side of the distant mountain.

"You don't have your skis on yet," Kyle said in a disappointed tone of voice.

"That's because I don't know how to put them on," Gillian answered squarely.

Kyle laughed and stuck his poles securely in the ground to keep them within reach while he helped Gillian struggle with her skis. Every time they thought she was finished, the boot snapped out of its moldings just as she went to move her ski, and they would have to begin again.

At last Gillian could shake each ski without having it fall off. Kyle reached for his poles, showing Gillian how to use them properly.

"Now we're off," he announced excitedly, pushing one

ski out in front of him and gliding forward smoothly. When Gillian tried to imitate him, she fell heavily to the ground and looked up pitifully at Kyle.

"Now do you believe me?" she asked. "I'm not going to be able to learn to ski."

"Nonsense," Kyle reassured her quickly and helped her up. "It'll take a little time and effort but you will learn. Now, to move across a flat surface, just treat your skis like cross-country skis and use the same motion."

Gillian took a deep breath and tried again. This time she moved a short distance. Although she was not at all graceful, she was moving. Kyle seemed to think that was enough.

They inched toward the tow lift, and Kyle explained to Gillian how to use it.

"It's very important that you don't sit on the tow lift. The seat will be T-shaped and more line will be released as pressure is exerted on it. If you just lean against it slightly and then let it pull you up the hill, it will work smoothly. If you sit on it, it will stretch farther and you'll fall off. It's just that simple."

Gillian gritted her teeth when it was their turn to step up to the contraption. The man behind Gillian and Kyle helped them get into position and then moved the tow bar toward them. At first Gillian was surprised because she didn't move. Suddenly the bar jerked them forward. Gillian fought with it for a moment and then fell over. When she struggled to her feet, her face was hot with embarrassment, and she quickly scrambled out of the path of the machine. Kyle had fought the imbalance but had fallen a short way farther up the hill. Gillian could see that he, too, looked a bit disgusted and embarrassed.

The man told them to step back toward him and he would help them again. Gillian was terrified that the same thing would happen. She was sure the idea worried Kyle, too, because he was very quiet.

When another bar came around and the man had helped them position themselves against it, Gillian prepared herself for the sudden jerk. This time she faltered for only a moment, and then they began to glide slowly up the hill. Gillian's knees were shaking and her eyes like saucers, but the two managed to make it the entire distance. She could sense that Kyle relaxed as they approached the crest of the hill.

Kyle held the rope for Gillian to push herself away and then let go of the bar to follow her. They turned at the top of the hill, and Gillian looked down the length of the slope Kyle had called the bunny hill. For a beginners' slope it looked terribly dangerous to Gillian.

"All right," Kyle said slowly, "it's time for your first skiing lesson. What you need to learn immediately is that you don't just let yourself fly straight down the hill. It's difficult to stop that way when you get to the bottom, and if you fall part of the way down, you can land in some very precarious positions.

"When you want to slow yourself down, you move your skis into the shape of an arrow, with the point directly in front of you. Then your skis will be working against the friction of the snow and you will slow down. This is called snowplowing. But you have to remember not to cross the tips of your skis. If you get them crossed, it's very difficult to uncross them and you can't help but fall. Do you think you're ready to try?"

Gillian certainly did not think she was, but she didn't think saying so would change anything, so she simply nodded slowly and closed her eyes.

"Follow me," Kyle called over his shoulder, "and you'd better open your eyes, too."

Gillian pushed herself forward and soon found that she was moving down the hill at a rate much faster than she wanted. She moved her skis quickly to form a snowplow and discovered that it was quite effective. She was so surprised that it worked that she looked up quickly to see if Kyle was watching. Suddenly she felt her skis slipping out of her control and in a moment she was lying flat in the snow, one loose ski gliding ahead of her down the hill.

"Not bad," Kyle called, catching the escaping ski. "You made it about twenty feet." When Gillian didn't return his laughter, Kyle changed the subject. "Now, if you want to turn while you're snowplowing, just put your weight on the foot opposite the direction you want to go and you'll move away from it."

Gillian crawled back on her feet while Kyle brought the ski and helped her put it back on. Determined not to fall again, she started down the hill, immediately positioning her feet in a snowplow. When she was sure she could manage to keep her skis in that position, she leaned onto her left ski slightly and was delighted to find herself veering to the right. When she shifted the weight to the right ski, she moved back to the left.

By this time they had reached the bottom of the hill, and Gillian was very excited about her accomplishment.

"Kyle," she cried, "I did it!"

Kyle cheered for her and they moved toward the tow lift once more. In no time at all, Gillian found that she had mastered the basic skills of skiing. She could snowplow, turn, and ride the tow lift gracefully—or at least all the way up the hill.

When lunchtime rolled around, Kyle had to almost force Gillian to come with him to the lodge for a bite to eat. She had been enjoying herself so much that she hadn't had time to think about how hungry she was getting.

"Hey, Gillian," Sharon's voice called. They turned to see her gliding toward them, leading a group of other staff members.

"I guess we all had the same idea about lunch. How do you like skiing so far?" Sharon asked, catching up to Gillian.

"I love it," Gillian answered enthusiastically. "It's not nearly as hard as I thought it would be." As they placed their skis and poles on the racks outside the lodge, Gillian told Sharon about her morning and they talked all through lunch.

Just as they were getting up from the table, Kate asked casually if Gillian would be moving to the longer slopes soon, and Gillian felt much of her confidence drain away at the thought.

When they had moved back outside and put their skis back on, Kyle approached Gillian.

"Would you be willing to move up to a more difficult slope?" he asked, and Gillian noticed the hopeful look in his eye.

"Why don't you go and I'll stay here for practice," Gillian answered brightly.

"No," Kyle sighed, "I promised not to leave you here by yourself and I won't. If we don't both go, then I won't go at all."

Gillian felt a pang of guilt for keeping Kyle away from the skiing he should be enjoying. "Okay," she whispered, "we'll go to another hill."

Kyle became as excited as if he had just been released from some sort of prison, and they moved forward more quickly.

"We have to ski down to the bottom of this hill to join the other lifts," Kyle explained. "They will take us to the top of that mountain ridge, and from there we can choose from a number of different trails."

Gillian followed close behind Kyle as he crossed toward the other lifts. These lifts were not tow bars but real chair-lifts. Gillian watched intently while other people took their place under the line and then were swept away by the lift.

She noticed that none of them seemed to be bothered by the process that left her trembling.

When it was time for Gillian to get on, she moved with Kyle and stood waiting for the chair to come around the pulley toward them. When it did, she sat down on it cautiously and held her breath. She had expected it to be more difficult than the other lift but found it was actually easier.

The ride up the mountain was very pleasant. For the first time Gillian took a good look at the area around her, marveling at the beauty—the clear blue sky and the white mountains rising against it. As the lift climbed higher up the mountainside, she could see more of the land around her. The long valley stretched out before her made the lodge look small and insignificant. Below her was a ski slope with only a few skiers. Scrutinizing it more closely, she could see large bumps covering the slope, and she supposed few people used it because of its poor condition.

When they reached the top, Gillian easily slid down the ramp away from the chair with Kyle right behind her.

"Here is a chart of the different slopes," Kyle said to Gillian, motioning her toward a large sign. From the sign, Gillian could look down the paths of two different trails, both looking quite treacherous to her.

"The difficulty of the trails is color coded," Kyle continued. "For instance, a green trail is much easier to ski than a black trail. We'll take the easiest one, over to our right."

Gillian followed him to the crest of the hill that began the slope. The view was magnificent. However, Gillian found it difficult to get caught up in its beauty when she was so close to the impossible task before her.

"Just relax and enjoy it," Kyle said softly. "You'll find that it's not as difficult as it looks."

As they moved down the slope, picking up speed, Gillian worked very hard at keeping control. At the bottom of this hill was a short incline and then another hill followed.

With the momentum they had built up coming down the first hill, they skied easily over the top of the next hill and began again.

With each hill, Gillian felt more at ease and began to enjoy it. She allowed herself to go faster and discovered she could still maintain control. When they emerged from a group of trees, Gillian realized they had reached the top of the bunny hill where she had started. She skied expertly down the slope and pulled up next to Kyle.

"Very nice," Kyle commented, smiling. "Would you like to try it again?"

"Sure," Gillian said confidently. "I'd like to."

The remainder of the day went by very quickly. Gillian learned more as the afternoon wore on and was amazed at how much she was enjoying herself. They tried different slopes. By the end of the day, they were tired and ready for the trip home.

Later that evening, Kyle walked Gillian back to her cabin and stood for a moment at the door. "I'm very proud of you," he said softly. "You not only learned quickly but you kept pressing yourself to do better. I admire that."

Gillian looked up at him and smiled. His eyes were fixed intently on her own and she noticed a look she had not seen before.

"I enjoyed myself very much," Kyle said warmly.

"I did too," Gillian responded.

For a minute they stood still, sensing the closeness of the moment. Then Kyle leaned forward and kissed her gently. When he moved away Gillian looked down demurely.

"I'm glad you came here, Miss Todd," he said. "You're very special."

Gillian looked back up at him breathlessly and smiled. "I'm glad I did, too," she answered.

"It took me far too long to realize just how special you

are. I hope I get a chance to make up for lost time."

Gillian blushed slightly and then breathed deeply. "I'd better turn in now. It was a big day," and without waiting for an answer, she retreated into her cabin and shut the door behind her.

Gillian leaned against the door and sighed deeply. She was so happy—yet just a little scared as well. Kyle was such a wonderful man, and she was beginning to have strong feelings for him. It was exciting to know that he was feeling the same way, but what would happen next?

22

$\mathcal{G}$illian rose extra early the next morning. It seemed as if the past day had been only a dream, but her aching body told her otherwise. It assured her she really had been skiing. Then the rest of her dreamlike day must have been reality as well. Kyle really had kissed her good-night.

It didn't take her long to get dressed in the chilly cabin and move close to the warming stove while she had her devotions. Before she had settled in the chair comfortably, there was a sharp knock on the door.

"Randy, you're up awfully early," she greeted the familiar face.

"John thought that there might be another storm, so I'm delivering food again." Then he added purposely, "Kyle can't do it because he might get a visitor today."

"Oh, really?" Gillian answered, unaffected. "Anyone I might know?"

"I doubt it," Randy continued, enjoying himself thoroughly. "She doesn't visit him very often—mostly she writes."

"She?" Gillian's eyebrows rose. "Who is 'she,' Randy?"

"He says she's just a friend from when he lived in Calgary—but who knows? Anyway, she's driving all the way from Lethbridge to visit him. I don't have many 'friends' that would do that for me."

Gillian was beginning to be annoyed with Randy's game. "But what is her name?"

"Trisha Meyer," came the curt reply.

"Well," Gillian stated, taking the bag of food from Randy, "thanks for dropping by. I'll see you later," and she firmly closed the door on the lopsided grin.

Wasn't that just like Randy? How he could provoke her! Well, she'd show him just how silly his gossip was. She'd just go right over and ask Kyle about Trisha herself. If he really was expecting a visitor, she would want to meet her anyway. If this whole thing was just another of Randy's stories, then she could dismiss it from her mind completely.

In a moment she was in her parka, hurrying down the trail to Kyle's cabin. When no one answered the knock at the door, Gillian set off toward the center of camp. If Kyle was really waiting for a visitor, it was very likely he would be in the lodge. That was usually the first place newcomers stopped when they arrived at the camp.

The front door of the lodge was unlocked, so Gillian stepped quickly inside, brushing at her pantlegs to loosen most of the snow before stepping onto the carpet. The shrill ring of a nearby telephone cut into the quiet around her, followed by an anxious, "Hello."

"Trisha!" Kyle's voice cried with obvious relief. "I was expecting you to be here by now. Where are you?" A long pause followed.

"How did you ever get way out there?" Another short pause. "Never mind, I'll come get you. It's not far, but give me at least twenty minutes in this snow. And don't worry. My truck will be able to pull you out of the drift with no problem. Can you stay with those folks for a few more minutes?" Another short pause. "Good. I'll be there just as soon as I can. Sit tight. Goodbye."

The receiver dropped back into place and Kyle shot out from behind a half-open office door, stopping short when he saw Gillian.

"Well, hello. What are you doing so far from your cabin on a day like this?"

"I—" Suddenly Gillian lost the words that had flowed in her mind only seconds before.

"Just wandering around, eh?" Kyle answered for her. "Well, I'd stay if I could but I have to run. Got to help out a friend who's in trouble."

"Kyle," Gillian called sharply before he could burst out into the chilly air, "Who's Trisha?" As soon as she had asked the question, she wished she could pull it back. That hadn't been how she'd planned to ask him.

"Oh, you heard me talking," came Kyle's answer, missing the intensity of the tone of her question. "She's a very good friend. And I want you to meet her just as soon as I bring her back. You'll love her just as much as I do. See you later." And he was gone.

For a moment Gillian stood rooted to the floor. Kyle had swept past her so quickly. There hadn't been time for explanations.

Well, that makes sense, she scolded herself. *This Trisha Meyer has gotten herself stuck in a snowdrift somewhere and he's in a hurry to pull her out. He'd do the same for you. Don't jump to any conclusions.* Suddenly she laughed. *Gillian, you actually took Randy seriously this morning. Don't you know him better than that? He's just a grown-up troublemaker and not worth listening to.*

Her reassuring thoughts gradually put her mind at ease. They made her realize she had been acting like some flighty girl in an old movie.

The more she thought about her fears, the sillier she felt. *I'd better go make them some hot chocolate and toast or something,* she told herself. *Trisha will be cold and probably hungry when she gets here.*

An hour went by before she heard someone entering

the dining hall. Gillian ran to greet them, disappointed when it was only John.

"Good morning, Gillian," he greeted her. "You're not making breakfast, are you? We're all eating in our own cabins today."

"No," she answered. "Trisha Meyer, Kyle's friend, got stuck on her way out here and he went to pull her out. I just thought they'd want something warm after being in the cold for so long."

"Good idea," he asserted. "So Kyle told you about Trisha, did he? I wondered if he'd had a chance. She's a real nice girl—pretty, too. You'll like her."

"Kyle said she was nice," Gillian answered evenly, choosing to ignore John's opinion of her looks.

"Yep, not many can pick 'em like Kyle can."

"Pick them?"

"Sure," John answered and then chuckled. "A man doesn't share himself like that with every woman who comes along. Well, Kate has a headache so she sent me all this way for an aspirin. I'd better get it and get going. Hey, I'll send Kyle and Trisha this way if I see them."

Gillian stood looking after John. *No, this can't be,* she assured herself. *John was joking. But what did he mean? What on earth was Kyle choosing to "share" with Trisha? It didn't make any sense.*

Forcefully pushing the thoughts from her mind, Gillian walked back to the kitchen and continued stirring the pot of hot chocolate absentmindedly. From far away, the sound of happy laughter drew nearer to the kitchen. Somehow it crept under Gillian's skin, making her angry without reason. Before she knew it she had slipped into her coat and shuffled out the back door. The way she was feeling, she doubted she could meet Trisha with a smile. Maybe if she went for a walk and calmed down, she would be able to be her cheerful self once more.

The snow crunched under her feet as she walked briskly down the path to her cabin. Somehow as she moved to close the door behind her, it slipped quickly from her fingers and slammed against its post, causing the window to shiver. Why had things suddenly become so complicated? She could deal with Randy's comments, but what had John meant?

23

"Gillian," called a voice from outside her door, rousing her from a fitful sleep in the armchair.

"Who is it?" she called back.

"It's Randy," came the answer.

Gillian rose reluctantly to open the door and squinted at the light reflecting off the snow. "Come on in," she invited sleepily.

"Just thought I'd come and check on you," Randy drawled, the enjoyment of his position obvious. "Didn't see you around today and I wondered if you were okay."

"I'm fine," Gillian answered curtly, adding in her mind, *or at least I was until now.*

"Should've stopped by sooner, but I had to saddle up a horse for Kyle's—uh—friend. They're sure making the rounds today. First showing her the whole camp, and then the woods." He paused. "Wonder what he wants to show her in the woods?" The words hung in the air.

"Randy, you're making too much of this. She's Kyle's friend—just a good friend."

"Don't know of too many 'good' friends I have who'd be hugging me all the time like she does Kyle."

Gillian spun on her heel and busied herself poking aimlessly into the fire. Randy, unheeding, followed her farther into the room.

"Nope, I sure don't have friends like that. I'm not saying I wouldn't want 'em, though. Kyle seems to enjoy it a lot."

"What do you want from me?" Gillian spat, whirling back to Randy. "Why are you telling me all this?"

"Well, now." Randy again became slow and deliberate. "Seems to me like you don't have too many choices."

"What do you mean?"

"Seems that Kyle has dumped you for this Trisha. 'Course, I could be wrong but . . ." he let the sentence linger.

"Oh, you think so, do you?" Gillian snapped. "And what exactly do you think my 'choices' are?"

"Well . . . you could probably try fighting for him, but that doesn't work very well. I think I have a better idea."

"And what's that?"

"I don't think he realizes that you don't belong to him. He's feeling pretty secure because you can't leave camp and all. Seems to me the old jealousy angle would do nicely here."

"What are you getting at, Randy?"

"I think that you and I ought to—well, you know what I mean," he said, taking another step closer, an eager twinkle in his eye. "The two of us ought to give him something to be jealous of."

"Get out!" Gillian's temper shot up. "Get out of this cabin and don't come back. If I see you near here again I'll— I'll call John. Get out!"

Randy's face clouded, but he backed quickly out the door, slamming it shut behind him.

The nerve! Gillian screamed inside of herself. *Who does he think he is? 'Let's make Kyle jealous.' You think I need you? I don't need your help—or anyone else's. If Kyle doesn't need me around when he's got Trisha, then . . . I'll just leave.*

It took a moment for the words to sink in. Yes, she would. She would leave camp. And Christmas would be the perfect opportunity—only a week and a half away. But could she really do it?

Determination crossed her face in an angry scowl. She grabbed her coat and thrust her arms into it, then burst out the door of her cabin and marched down the path to the center of camp.

The call to make a plane reservation seemed to be the easiest step, so she hurried into her office and dialed the phone. Before long she emerged again, shaken slightly by the suddenness of her plan. There had been only one flight unfilled, and it was to leave the following day. The man had told her that this was open only because of a cancellation and he encouraged her to book the seat immediately. She had only planned to check on the flights, but at this news she had gone ahead and made the reservation.

John was working over a stack of papers when she entered his office. It was perhaps the most difficult thing she had ever done to try to make him understand that she wanted to leave. At first he agreed quickly, anticipating that she was only asking for the holiday season off. When she made it clear that she was considering the possibility of not returning, at least for a while, he seemed confused. At last she convinced him that she was going, making a vague attempt at an explanation. It was evident to her that he believed she was leaving only out of homesickness. He kept assuring her that if she changed her mind after she had been home for a couple of days, her job would still be open.

At last she left his office and scurried back to her cabin. When she arrived she moved stiffly to the bedroom and threw her suitcase onto the bed, then crumpled in a heap beside it and began to cry.

"Oh, Jake," she sobbed, "what am I doing?"

———

For the most part, Gillian spent the next day in her cabin. The news had not yet begun to filter through the camp that she was leaving, so she was able to spend the time alone. That afternoon, after stopping to say goodbye to a very confused Sharon and Kate, she placed her suitcase in the waiting car and stood impatiently watching for John to arrive and drive her to the bus station. Before too long she saw him striding across the snowy path toward her.

"Sorry I'm late," he hurried. "There's been a change of plans. Randy is going to have to take you because I have to meet with some businessmen today. I forgot about it earlier."

"You're sure Randy's the only one who can take me?" Gillian pleaded.

"Yes. Is that a problem?"

"I—I guess not. Where is he?"

"He'll be along in just a minute," he said, beginning to move away. Then he added meaningfully, "Now, don't forget to call me in a couple days—just to see how long you've decided to stay."

Gillian nodded anxiously, watching the paths around her for movement. She wasn't certain whether she was watching for Randy or just a glimpse of Kyle, but she held her breath expectantly.

At last Randy rounded the corner, and Gillian sighed deeply. No, he hadn't been the one she had wanted to see.

"Hello," he called cordially.

"Hi," Gillian answered unenthusiastically.

"Ready to go?"

"Well, I didn't really say goodbye to anyone," she struggled. "Maybe I should do that quickly."

"Kyle's not around."

Gillian turned toward him. "Where is he?"

"Out with Trisha. They went ice fishing today," he answered, purposely leaving out the fact that he himself had sent them.

"I guess he didn't know I was leaving," she muttered quietly.

"Sure he did," Randy returned. "I told him myself."
Again he omitted the details of just what he had told Kyle.

"And he didn't even try to tell me goodbye?" came the incredulous question.

"Guess not."

Randy's sharp answers were annoying Gillian, but not as much as his face. It told clearly how anxious he was to give them.

Looking straight into his eyes, she stated firmly, "Randy, if you're the only one around to drive me to the station, I guess I'll have to take what I can get—but only on one condition. Don't you dare say one word for the rest of the trip! Don't you so much as cough. I'm tired of your schemes and opinions. Just keep it all to yourself. Do you hear me?"

"Sure," he muttered and threw himself into the seat, waiting for Gillian to climb in on the other side. What did it matter? He had already said all he planned to say.

The drive was slow and painful. Gillian remembered the place where she and Kyle had spotted the deer on her first trip with him. There had also been other times when they had traveled the road. Each of these came back to her now with painful memories. One question kept ringing in her mind. If he knew she was leaving, why hadn't he come to say goodbye? Randy may not have been much of a friend lately, but how could he have lied about that? Kyle had simply not shown up.

At last they pulled into the bus station and climbed stiffly from the car. There was no sign of the bus yet, so they moved inside the run-down building to wait. Before many minutes had gone by, a car sped down the road and pulled sharply up to the depot. Gillian gasped as Kyle jumped out.

"Kyle!" she and Randy exclaimed at the same time. Then Gillian ran out to him.

"Why are you leaving?" he asked, searching her face for the truth.

Awkwardness came over Gillian. "I—I need to go home. I just have to go."

Kyle placed his hands on her shoulders and looked deeply into her eyes. "Gillian," he asked softly, "I want the truth. Did you really ask to be given 'space'—and time alone to sort your feelings?"

"What!" she cried. "Where on earth did you get that idea?"

In one motion the two of them turned to look inside the depot, but Randy was nowhere in sight. "What did he tell you?" Kyle asked, beginning to see the humor in the situation.

"That you and Trisha were—more than just friends."

"Well, we are. I thought you knew about that."

Gillian pulled back sharply and Kyle hurried to explain. "I guess you didn't find my note then. I left it in your office yesterday afternoon. I thought you were working all day or I would have stopped by your cabin myself. Randy told me you were busy. Anyway, two years ago, when I was living in Calgary, Trisha was in the hospital with terrible kidney problems. I heard about her through my church. A group of us felt we should do something for her so we agreed that whoever was found compatible would donate a kidney. That's what the scar on my side is from, remember? You commented on it when we went canoeing." The light was beginning to dawn in Gillian's confused mind. "Anyway, Trisha recovered and we became very close. She was even led to the Lord through the whole experience and we've kept in touch. It's an awesome feeling knowing that a part of me has kept her alive for these last two years. It's really made us both learn a lot." He paused. "I should have taken the time to explain that much earlier. The note was a poor attempt at best. I should never have listened to Randy. If I'd had any idea that it would lead to this, I—I would have never let you—

"Where is Randy, anyway? He's got a lot of explaining to do."

"Forget it, Kyle," Gillian laughed suddenly. "We should have been smart enough not to trust anything that came out of his mouth. It's our fault. I'm just glad that it's over."

"Me, too. Can I drive you back?"

"Oh, but I have to go see my folks. They already know I'm coming and they'd be so disappointed."

"I guess," Kyle answered slowly. He looked at her, quickly making a decision. "But then I'll have to give you your Christmas present early."

Purposefully, Kyle reached inside his coat and pulled out a small box. Then he chuckled, "This is for you. Would you believe that Trisha helped me pick it out?"

Gillian snapped open the lid and the glimmer of a diamond burst from the center of a dainty ring.

"I know it seems rash, but I've never been more certain about a decision before. I've spent a great deal of time in prayer, and I'm sure you have too. But I have to ask you now before anything else happens. Gillian, will you marry me?" She heard the question from a million miles away. *Is this really happening?* At last she faced him, tears in her eyes.

"I'm so stupid, Kyle. Here I am running and acting like a schoolgirl, and yet you want to marry me! Do you know what you're in for?"

"That's exactly why I asked," he returned with deep feeling. "I know I'll never get another chance like this. There's no one else in this world that could take your place in my heart. Gillian, I love you."

And then she was in his arms, being held the way she had longed for. "Yes," she whispered against his cheek,

"I've been praying, too. Praying for so long that you'd love me someday."

The bus pulled into the driveway at that moment and Gillian pulled herself away from Kyle's kiss. "I wish we had more time," she whispered.

"We have all the time in the world. We have the rest of our lives."

24

"Mom, Dad!" Gillian called across the airport. "I missed you both so much."

"Welcome home, darling," came the happy reply.

The days went by quickly and pleasantly. Gillian told her parents about her engagement, and they laughed together about how it happened.

"It sounds like he is a very fine man," Mrs. Todd agreed. "I'm happy for you, dear. Perhaps your father and I can find some time this winter for a visit up there."

"Could you?" cried Gillian, noting the shine in her father's eyes. He would finally get to see Canada again.

"We'll be there," he assured her.

———

"You seem different, Gillian," her mother mentioned a short time later. "And I don't think it's just experience. You're more helpful and good-natured than before. Love must suit you well."

"I am different, Mom," she answered, trying to find the right words to explain her new faith in God without offending her mother. "I became a Christian while I was at the camp."

"Don't be silly, dear. You were a Christian before you went. We're all Christians."

"But that's not what I mean. I learned that being a Christian is more than just growing up in a so-called Christian nation. It's a personal commitment each person has to choose to make—not one that your family passes on to you."

"Gillian, what are you talking about? Our family has always supported the church and attended regularly on all of the major holidays. We live like good people. What more can you mean?"

Gillian prayed a quick prayer as she struggled for just the right words to make her mother understand. "I know you believe in the Bible, Mom, but do you know that it says, 'Except a man be born again, he cannot see the kingdom of God'? That verse means that unless we take a step of faith on our own and ask Christ into our hearts and our lives, we haven't done enough. That's why it is so important that I found God at the camp. It's made such a difference in the way I feel and think. I was shown by lots of people that God wants to be a personal God. That He loves me enough to want to get to know me. So much, in fact, that He sent His Son to die for me. And I do know Him now."

"Yes, you told me in your letter how that man, I think his name was Jake, talked to you all the time about praying to be 'saved.' Do you really think it changed anything?"

"It's hard to explain, but when I pray to God now it's not like when I was little or all those times when I was in trouble. Now I can tell Him about everyday things and I know that He cares. And I realize now how important it is to ask for His forgiveness. I know that lots of people think it's enough just to try to be good, that if we make some kind of effort God will just automatically take pity on us and forgive us. It's not true. God wants to forgive us, but He can't until we ask."

"I've heard Sandy Johnson talk about being a Christian that way, but I thought it was all in her head. You say it really has made a difference for you?"

"It really has. I care about people more now than I used

to. Before I didn't spend much time thinking about how other people felt, but now it's like I have a deeper love for them. Oh, sometimes I'm still tempted to feel selfish, but I can deal with it—at least most of the time. I know that with God's help I can overcome those feelings and do the right thing."

"Well, I wouldn't have taken you very seriously, I'm afraid, if I hadn't seen how different you are. I'm still a little confused, but I'll do some thinking about it."

"I'm glad, Mom. I want you and Dad, more than anyone else, to know Christ. You'll never regret it."

———————

Later that day, Krystal stopped by and the two had time to talk alone. Gillian told her all about Kyle and their relationship. Krystal laughed when she heard how they met and how much Gillian had thought she disliked Kyle then. The scene at the bus station almost brought a tear to her eye.

"He must really love you, Jill. I'm glad he caught you before you left." Suddenly she burst out, "Oh, I brought something for you. It was going to be just a silly gag, but I guess it means a lot more now, considering—" Krystal stopped midsentence and rummaged through her purse. "Here it is," she announced triumphantly and held a small object up in the air.

"What on earth is that?" Gillian asked, trying to see what Krystal was waving.

"Shut your eyes," Krystal teased, "or I won't let you see it."

Gillian gave in and closed her eyes. She felt Krystal place a hard round disc in her hand and when she opened her eyes she recognized it. It was a bus token.

"Don't you remember?" Krystal laughed, when she saw Gillian's confused expression. "Your valedictorian speech. The bus token," she prodded further.

"Sure, I remember, but what does that have to do with us now?"

"You said in your speech that each of us has earned a bus token. As far as I can see, you've already gone a good distance on yours. I hope the rest of us can be so brave."

At last Gillian understood the point Krystal was trying to make. She looked down at the hard plastic circle in her hand and thought seriously about her words.

"I guess I didn't realize what I was really saying back then," Gillian finally said aloud.

"None of us did," Krystal said, "but we're learning. Just like anyone else who has the will to learn."

It was clear to her now. Gillian hadn't known then as she knew now that her life had a definite purpose and a well-designed plan. God had used the words that once meant very little to show her an important lesson. The only certain way to win is to trust the One who holds the plan. Only then is a life completely full.

Gillian thought of what her life would be if she had not taken that first step. She would never have met Kyle or Jake or Sharon, and most importantly, she might never have come to know God.

"Thanks, Krystal," she whispered softly, "I guess I wasn't so foolish back then, after all."